23

1960

WHERE ELSE BUT

ALASKA?

Other Stories of ALASKA

FRED MACHETANZ

PANUCK, ESKIMO SLED DOG

ON ARCTIC ICE

SARA AND FRED MACHETANZ

BARNEY HITS THE TRAIL

RICK OF HIGH RIDGE

All illustrated by Fred Machetanz

WHERE ELSE BUT

ALASKA?

BY SARA MACHETANZ

LITHOGRAPHS AND PHOTOGRAPHS BY FRED MACHETANZ

CHARLES SCRIBNER'S SONS · NEW YORK

TO WEEGAH

CONTENTS

WHERE ELSE BUT

ALASKA?

TRAILMATES

CHAPTER I

WELCOME TO UNALAKLEET

THE PLANE ROARED OUT over the frozen Bering Sea, banked steeply into the wind and started down. Far below, a few scattered buildings burrowed in the snow of a wind-blown sandspit. This was Unalakleet, an Alaskan Eskimo village. It was also where I would be married to a man I had met six months before while traveling through the territory.

The plane taxied to a stop and the airline hostess, dressed in a white fur parka, unlatched the door. "We're here," she said, smiling. Whereupon the entire passenger list for that day stepped down and into Fred's arms.

As I glanced over his shoulder, I was amazed to see a milling crowd of parka-clad Eskimos, laughing children and barking dogs. After flying over two snow-covered mountain ranges and miles and miles of desolate muskeg and tundra, so much activity was the last thing I expected.

Another surprise was several white faces looking out of fur ruffs. They were Civil Aeronautics Administration employees who lived at the air strip and issued around-the-clock weather reports to pilots.

Fred introduced me to the Eskimo postmaster Frank Ryan, who was busy unloading mail and reloading cargo on to his dog sled. "Pleased to meet you," he repeated several times pumping my hand up and down. Next we went over to a receiving line of six smiling Eskimo women dressed in bright cloth-covered fur parkas. They were several inches shorter than my five-and-a-half feet, with shiny olive complexions and black eyes and hair.

"This is Sara," Fred said.

They all grinned widely and offered their hands. "How do! How do!" and, to Fred, "*Ah-ree-gah!*" (very nice).

They watched closely while Fred fashioned a makeshift seat for me in his dog sled. As they realized what he was doing, they burst into unrestrained giggling. I suppose it did seem funny to them that I was going for a dog team ride wearing open-toed pumps and a feather-puff hat. But when Fred had written "Use your own judgment" in advising me what to wear, he had given my so-called judgment much more credit than it deserved.

The cold was unbearable. My nose, fingers and toes were numb and I could not keep from shaking. "How cold is it?" I asked through teeth clattering like a telegrapher's key.

"Oh about 35°."

"BELOW?"

Fred nodded and then I *was* cold.

He helped me into the sled, suggesting I sit on my feet, then, giving the dogs a starting "All right," jumped on the runners at the back. We were off. While we drove the half mile into the village, he held his fur mitts over my ears. I tried to warm my face with my hands but before this had any effect my hands started freezing, so I put them inside my coat again. We whizzed along between low-lying foothills barren of trees on our left and the frozen Bering Sea on our right.

"How's Mr. Traeger?" I asked.

Mr. Traeger was Fred's uncle. He had first come to Alaska as a prospector in 1898. Failing to make a strike, he had established a Trading Post at Unalakleet, and it was here Fred stayed when in Eskimo country.

"Uncle Charlie's fine," Fred answered. "He gave us the dogs. They're a good team."

They were running in a steady jog, with tails high, and they seemed to be enjoying every step. Their teeth bared in panting almost gave the appearance of laughing.

The ride wasn't smooth. To get into Unalakleet, we had to cross one snowbank after another, ranging as high as twelve feet. I forgot to warm my hands and clung desperately to the sled while we crashed over the banks and rocked from side to side. Eskimos waved to us from their log homes and sled dogs chained near by set up a howling chorus of welcome. We hurtled over the eighth bank and into a level square.

"Haw, Haw!" Fred yelled at the dogs, and, as we turned left, "There's your future home."

Ahead was a sprawling, two-story building covered with sheet iron. Large painted letters identified it as the "Unalakleet Post Office" and, underneath, "Charles A. Traeger—General Merchandise." A tremendous snow drift reached to windows all across the second floor.

"Whoa!" Fred stopped the dogs and led me through a shed protecting the front door into the downstairs of the Post. The room we came into was quite dark, like a friendly old barn, but instead of the odor of hay and horses there was a pungent blend of furs, seal oil and wood fires.

The first object to catch my eye was a big cast-iron stove in the center of the room. Logs the size of cross-ties were

stacked beside it. On either side, shelves sagged under a winter's supply of canned foods, lamps, bolts of cloth and hardware. Reindeer and wolf skins hung from the rafters while stacked traps and rifles gave evidence of the means by which they were obtained.

At the rear of the Trading Post was the Post Office, looking surprisingly as if it had just come from a country store.

We climbed the stairs leading to a roomy kitchen with a banquet-sized table and an ancient oil-burning range. There was an archway between the kitchen and an outsized living room with many windows.

A big man came forward. He had a strong, smooth-shaven face, and eyes reflecting the blue of the ice he had looked out on so long.

"Sara, this is Uncle Charlie."

His hand swallowed mine. "Welcome to Unalakleet!" Then he added, "and to the family."

"Thank you, Uncle Charlie." I knew we would get along, for, although he was a rugged individual in a rough country, his voice and smile told me he was a gentle, sensitive man.

He took my coat. "You're going to have to get some different clothes—say," he leaned toward me for a closer look, "your ear is frostbitten."

My hand flew up to feel whether or not my ear had dropped off and I ran to the kitchen mirror. I stared with terror at the lobe, which was paper-white.

"Will . . . will I lose it?" I asked trying to sound offhand, as if walking around with half an ear were the most common thing in the world.

Uncle Charlie shook his head and laughed. "Of course not. If that happened every time you get frostbitten, I wouldn't have a face by now. We'll get you a parka so it won't happen again. Want to wash up?"

He showed me the system.

Water was drawn from two tremendous hogsheads set on a low shelf. Each morning they were filled with great chunks of ice cut out of the Unalakleet River. There was always hot water in two kettles on the stove and he cautioned me whenever I poured any out, to refill them immediately for the next user.

The "sink" was an enamel bowl set in the hole of a shelf, with a five gallon bucket underneath to catch the used water. Water was a precious item here, since every drop had to be melted down from sled loads of ice that were at three dollars per load.

"I'll show you the Trading Post if you want," Fred offered. First he took me to the guest room, which would soon be our living quarters. It was larger than the average bedroom but as crowded as a freight depot with Fred's camera equipment and painting supplies. A single path led through the boxes to a bed in one corner. Another path led to an oil stove and another to one of two windows.

As our inspection progressed, I reached the conclusion that Uncle Charlie was a Sourdough who refused to compromise with his environment. He had installed every possible comfort for himself and offered what he could to the natives. One innovation had been windchargers to generate electricity for radios.

"Do you mean the Eskimos have radios?" I asked unbelieving.

"Sure. They're crazy about Western and hillbilly ballads."

The Trading Post was wired for electricity, but shortly before my arrival, the windchargers had broken, so gasoline lamps and a battery radio had been pressed into service. In a back storage room off the kitchen was a kerosene refrigerator to keep food warm in winter and cold in summer.

Against the walls of the big front room were half-a-dozen army cots. Since there were no accommodations for wayfarers in the village, Uncle Charlie maintained a boarding house in conjunction with his Trading Post. It was not a profitable enterprise, but when any stranger was without a place to stay Uncle Charlie would not turn him away. The walls were almost sagging from the weight of many calendars.

"Each salesman brings Uncle Charlie a calendar and he has to hang it up so as not to hurt his feelings," Fred explained.

In Uncle Charlie's corner, partitioned off the main room

with curtains, there was a bed with an innerspring mattress, shelves loaded with well-worn books and a battle-scarred victrola.

While we talked Oswald Paneok, who doubled as house-boy and clerk in the Trading Post, filled the barrel of oil feeding the kitchen stove. Next, he took out the "catch" buckets under the faucets of the hogsheads to water the dogs. Then the five gallon tin under the sink had to be emptied. He returned loaded with wood for the living room stove and as he went out took along the gasoline lamps to fill. I knew I would never again flick a light switch, turn a faucet or set a thermostat without a feeling of wonder. Still, while we were in Eskimoland, there was never any worry of frozen pipes or electrical failures.

Another Eskimo came into the kitchen.

"Solovelik!" Fred shouted in a mock serious voice that told me these two were good friends. "Come meet my bride-to-be."

The little old man stood before us hopping, birdlike, from one foot to another.

"Sara, this is Stevan Ivanoff. He's the United States Commissioner and the best cook on the Bering Sea Coast."

"How do! How do!" Stevan quivered with joy. His beady eyes glistened with eagerness, his hands rubbed together in an overflow of delight.

"Will you be home this afternoon?" Fred asked.

"Yes, yes," Stevan nodded his head in frantic approbation.

"We'll come over and get our marriage license, then."

"That good. Good, good," Stevan said, and, smiling and nodding, he backed from the room.

In a very short time, Stevan had an excellent meal ready for us. We all sat down to the big table loaded with potatoes, corn bread, stewed cabbage, canned fruit, cookies and salmon trout fresh from the Unalakleet River. It was all delicious, but I would have probably savored each bite even more had I known I was eating our last cabbage until after the boat came, in June.

Fred and I were full of talk of all the things that had happened in the four months we'd been apart and—much more important—the wedding. Because I had known absolutely nothing of protocol in Eskimoland, I had left everything entirely to him.

Uncle Charlie remained quiet throughout the meal. I didn't know whether he was thinking he might have known this same happiness, or whether he just wasn't used to having a white woman around after fifty years of bachelor life.

When Solovelik excused himself to do the dishes, the scarcity of water was again demonstrated. His dish water was the rinse water very carefully saved from the breakfast washing. Then he left us while I dug out the jacket I had included in my trousseau—"protection," the clerk had assured me, "in 40° below weather."

Fred was dubious.

"I don't believe that will keep you warm. The rayon lining will hold the moisture of your body. If you were out on trail, you'd freeze."

But I was adamant. I was going to wear it. And I would not accept the long woolen underwear Uncle Charlie suggested.

'Not those horrors,' I thought inwardly. 'I'll freeze first.'

I did tie a scarf over my head to protect my ears, and put on the fur boots Fred had sent for Christmas. He gave me some dried grass to tuck underneath the insoles for insulation, just as the Eskimos did.

We stepped out of the shed and a blast of cold wind hit us. It cut through my woolen slacks and "forty below" jacket as if they had blown away with the first puff. I caught my breath but I knew Fred was watching, so I made no complaint on the short walk to Stevan's cabin.

Fred pushed the door of the outer room open. It was crammed with dog harnesses, boots, parkees and was in addition to being a storage room, an indoor toilet. There were outhouses in the village to be sure, but when the thermometer rested at minus 30° or so, snow-covered paths leading to them remained unsullied by human feet.

The man who met us at the door might have been a total stranger. He was exceedingly dignified, as befitted the only force of law and order in Unalakleet. In deep tones he presented his wife and daughter, Emily, who had gone "outside" to college and was now teaching in the local school.

Solemnly, Stevan pointed for us to sit on the bed, then, twitching his walrus mustache in concentration, he filled out the necessary blanks for our license. When he had finished, he stood up and very gravely shook hands and showed us to the door. The transition was unbelievable. I wondered if all Eskimos were so formal in their homes. I soon learned they weren't, for we called on another family that afternoon, but not before I asked Fred to take me by the Trading Post so I could change into Uncle Charlie's fur parka and long underwear.

Comfortably clothed, I could enjoy the walk. Looking around, I noticed first a second-story-level village of little houses built on stilts. They were caches, used for storing skins and food out of reach of prowling animals. We passed fish-drying racks looking like the skeletons of cabins and dog barns half dug out of the ground and divided into stalls.

Homes were low and usually had one or at the most, two rooms. All of the cabins in the village faced toward the South, away from the constant east-west wind which was responsible for the many snowdrifts.

We stopped before one of them. It was the home of Mr. and Mrs. Oliver. Their family included a son, Nathan, two grown daughters, a grandchild and Mrs. Oliver's mother, Kyrok.

"Yah! Yah! (Welcome, Welcome)." They all crowded to the door to shake hands.

Mrs. Oliver put the kettle on for tea while Kyrok motioned for me to sit beside her on the bed. She was old enough to remember when Alaska was sold to the United States by Russia, but like many great-grandparents in the village, she could neither speak nor understand English. Still, we had a fine conversation as she patted my hand.

The grandchild crawling on the floor was openly adored by all members of the family. Eskimo children are seldom punished by their parents, who defer to an ancient belief that the soul of the last person to die in the village enters the next born.

We all sat down to the table for tea served with home-made bread, low-bush cranberry jam and seal oil. Seal oil took the place of butter, but, instead of spreading it, the first two fingers were dipped in and conveyed directly to the mouth.

"So, Fred, you got woman?" Mrs. Oliver started the conversation.

"Is she strong?" Mr. Oliver sent an appraising glance in my direction.

"She's strong," Fred assured them. At any other time I would have considered this a questionable attribute but here it seemed to be highly desirable, for they all nodded in satisfaction.

"You get baby, now," Mrs. Oliver looked significantly at me.

"How's trapping?" Fred changed the subject.

"Good," Nathan replied. "I get lotsa blankets." These

were the large beaver skins. "I go out again when dog's feet well." He went on to explain that his dogs' paws had been cut by ice on the last trip. "Next time I take boots for them."

Mrs. Oliver had been sewing on the new equipment when we arrived. She held up little boots made from heavy drill to which ties had been attached.

The talk went on, for the Eskimos were gregarious and liked nothing better than a tea party. When finally they waved us off with *"Bee-rah-itic"* (Good-bye to you two) and we had replied *"Bee-rah-itchee"* (Good-bye to you all) night had come.

It was so cold the snow crunched underfoot but we didn't notice, for the sky was lit up like the Fourth of July. I had seen Northern Lights before—pale yellow-green curtains undulating across the sky. But tonight as if sensing a special occasion, streamers of pink, lavender, green and yellow arched to the zenith of the heavens.

"The Eskimos say if you whistle they'll come closer," Fred told me.

I started whistling, but the Northern Lights didn't alter their course one whit. Perhaps I failed to come up with the correct tune.

Suddenly the air began to fill with a strange low moan increasing in volume as it spread throughout the village. It was the sled dogs' yearning cry—primitive, eerie and straight from the heart of the northern night. Just as suddenly and all at once, it stopped, but for me, as for anyone who has lived in the far North, it became forever an exact expression of the Great Alone.

The sled dogs themselves grew to be much more than a

symbol, as I came to know them. However, that was a little later.

The next day was taken up with preparations. Uncle Charlie, Fred and I went to call at the home of the missionary directly across the square. On our way we passed the large, yellow frame school, which housed the two white teachers and the nurse. These three buildings on the square—the mission home, the school and the Trading Post represented the leading forces in the majority of Eskimo villages.

The Reverend Emory Lindgren and his pretty blonde wife looked little older than college students, yet they had been doing mission work in Alaska for five years and their two children had been born there. Fred's best man, Lowell Anagik, who clerked at the Trading Post, and another friend of the family, Eula Kootuck, who was to be my maid-of-honor, were waiting too.

Since there had never been a wedding in the church at Unalakleet, during Mr. Lindgren's stay, we had no precedent to follow. Emory took down a shiny new book of etiquette and a thumb-worn Bible from the shelf. With brown eyes serious in his young face, he read of white gloves, boutonnieres, canopies and limousines. Before he had finished, we were all laughing. Emily Post had certainly not covered the fine points of marriage in an Eskimo village.

We all trooped over to the mission for a rehearsal followed by a lively discussion as to whether or not we should wear shoes, since the 30° below cold spell remained unbroken. We finally decided to wear our boots, carry our shoes and put them on before going up the aisle.

While all of this was going on, the Eskimo women of the

village were busy making an archway and a bridal bouquet of red, yellow and blue waxed crepe paper roses. Extra ice had to be gathered and melted down for coffee. Uncle Charlie brought out one of the frozen turkeys that had arrived on the last boat before freeze-up. Mrs. Lindgren baked a wedding cake.

That night we hauled out the wash-tubs to melt ice for baths. I found that adding bubble powder made the water go much farther, but was unable to decide whether the most efficient method was to kneel and expose three feet of myself vertically or sit and expose arms and legs horizontally. Whatever position was chosen could not be maintained for more than a few swipes of the wash cloth, since the encompassing cold made it necessary to rotate in the heat from the oil stove. With each banging of elbows, bruising of knees and burning of flesh, the function rapidly lost its importance.

On the morning of the wedding I slept late and according to convention did not see Fred, who had gone to Lowell's until the ceremony.

Stevan was busy in the kitchen preparing the turkey.

"Good morning," I greeted him.

"How do."

I walked to the window. "It looks like a pretty day."

"Yah. *Kee-rah-chee-ok.*"

"What does that mean?"

"It mean sunshine."

"*Kee-rah-chee-ok!*" I could almost have guessed from the joyful sound of the word.

Now and then Eskimo women hurried across the square

carrying waxed crepe paper flowers to the mission. Their decorating was done before an audience Stevan declared had sat from mid-morning to be assured of seats at the two o'clock ceremony. Children ran excitedly about although two announcements had been made at church services that anyone under fifteen was to be kept home because of limited seating capacity. But school had been turned out because the teachers wanted to come! A notice on the door of the nurse's office announced there were to be no emergencies that afternoon so she might attend. Everyone not on duty at the CAA Station hiked in to swell the ranks of guests.

"It not like old time Eskimo marriage," Stevan was standing beside me watching.

"How was that?" I asked.

"All a fella do then was see girl. Like her, tell his parents. If they like girl, Mother make fine parkee and boots for her. She take these to girl's parents. If it all right with them, girl wear parkee and boots whether it all right with girl or not. When fella see girl wear his parkee and boots, she his woman."

It sounded wonderfully simple and attractive at the time.

Stevan finished basting the turkey and gave a final turn to the ice cream freezer and left for the mission. Uncle Charlie had not put in an appearance all morning, so I was completely alone. I thought longingly of my family five thousand miles away, but it was with the wish they were in Unalakleet rather than my being back with them. My wedding could be in no other place for I was marrying not only a man but a country, as surely as if "trust, honor and love Alaska" were a part of the vows.

While I was finishing dressing, the mission bell began to ring to let anyone who had missed the word know that something unusual was in the offing.

At five minutes to two, Uncle Charlie came for me. With shoes in hand, we proceeded the 150 yards to the mission vestibule. Eula was already there, taking off her boots.

A few wheezy notes of Schubert's Serenade floated back to us. Then, interspersed with deeper wheezes and thumps from the little upright organ, a recognizable version of the wedding march filled the air. Eula started up the aisle. Uncle Charlie took me on his arm and into the main room of the mission. For a fleeting second, I thought of a sunflower garden, as row on row of fur parka ruffs turned toward us. I imagine the walk to the altar has always seemed long, but I am certain mine was made longer by the limitations of our organ.

It was a double ring ceremony. I heard the passage we had selected from Ruth. "Whither thou goest, I will go; and where thou lodgest, I will lodge; thy people shall be my people . ." and at exactly 2:08, Monday, January 27, Fred and I were pronounced man and wife.

We rushed to the vestibule, put on our boots and ran to the Trading Post, where Fred carried me over the doorstep. We had hardly removed our wraps before the village started to arrive en masse—old men, old women, mothers with babies on their backs and strong hunters who would much prefer facing an angry wolverine to this party.

They all filed into the living room and sat in a large, silent circle on the floor, feet straight front. I quailed upon entering that arena of strange faces, but once Fred and I started around shaking hands, everyone relaxed and began to talk.

Over and over, I heard the word *"Ogoik."* When we came to Stevan, he greeted me with *"Ogoik."*

"What does *'Ogoik'* mean?" I asked.

"It mean 'daughter-in-law of the village,' " he explained. "Traeger, good father. Fred his son. Now, you daughter-in-law."

I was deeply pleased, for I very much wanted to be accepted among the Eskimos as Fred was.

For a special treat, they began to sing a hymn, first in English, then in native. After this solemn note, Uncle Charlie brought out a crate of oranges which he tossed to the youngsters lined up on the snowbank outside the windows. Cookies, ice cream and coffee were served to the guests. Mrs. Lindgren's beautiful wedding cake was set on a card table in the center of the room and equipped with a butcher knife the size of a bolo. Fred and I cut it in traditional style. We cut it down to the last crumb and it was quite a feat, because every one of our two hundred and fifty guests had a taste.

Following the reception, Uncle Charlie gave a turkey dinner for the wedding party and servers. We were all sitting around the kitchen table talking and laughing when without warning a shower of rice descended. There was great merriment as we picked the grains out of our hair and Fred emptied his pockets and the cuffs of his pants.

Suddenly he wheeled at one of the laughing Eskimo girls. *"EE-loo-rok!"* he shouted.

Vigorously she shook her head and everyone burst out laughing all over again.

"Ee-loo-rok" was a relationship rather than a name. It came into being when two Eskimos made jokes on one another. This right of mutual prank-playing was recognized and approved by all the villagers. Thus Fred and Lilly as *"Ee-loo-roks"* had been victimizing each other for years and providing a great deal of fun all around. The custom was so strongly established that *"Ee-loo-roks"* were handed down through the generations. To me, *"Ee-loo-rok"* exploded the myth that Eskimos were a phlegmatic people devoid of a sense of humor.

After the guests went home, Uncle Charlie ducked into his curtained corner and brought out two beautiful rabbit-fur parkas with matching boots for our wedding present. The ruffs of wolf and wolverine were handsomely thick, in addition to being moisture-repellent.

I slid into mine and paraded about. "They're gorgeous, Uncle Charlie."

"They certainly are well made," Fred looked up from studying the intricate border design. "I'll bet Miowak sewed them."

"She did," Uncle Charlie smiled.

"Who's Miowak?"

"She's my foster mother," Fred told me. "She adopted me into her family when I first came to the village. There was no air strip in those days and my pilot landed out on the tundra. The Eskimos weren't accustomed to airplanes then, so everyone in the village turned out to see the 'big bird' from the sky. Miowak was there, too. Just a year before I arrived, her son, who was part white, had died and when she saw me step off the plane, she thought I was he returned to life. I didn't know it at the time, but she was so emotionally upset she nearly fainted. Even after she knew better, she still regarded me as her son and invited me to her home and did nice things for me. She made an entree for me into village life that couldn't have been acquired in any other way, because she treated me as one of her family."

I looked at Fred and realized there were things to be learned about my new husband as well as the people and this country I had come to.

ACHEBUK, THE SEAL HUNTER

Chapter II

SUB-ZERO PHOTOGRAPHY

W E WERE HAVING A HARD WINTER or "Man Winter" as the Eskimos said. The temperature continued between 30° and 40° below without a break.

We decided to postpone our honeymoon by dog team until early spring, when the Northbound sun would make longer days and more agreeable traveling weather.

Meanwhile Fred thought it a good idea for me to meet the dogs and learn how to drive them. When we first came into the dimly-lit shed where they were housed, their frenzied half howls and their huge size frightened me.

"They won't hurt you," Fred assured me. "Look, their tails are wagging. Take off your mitt and let them smell your hand."

I did. Instead of biting it off at the wrist the dogs gave a few tentative sniffs and then a friendly lick. All of the straining at the chains and noise was nothing more than excitement at the prospect of going on trail.

We took Blackie out first. He was large (about 70 pounds) with a strong, well-built frame and a fierce look. As leader, he held the towline straight while the other four dogs were fastened in pairs behind him. This done, Fred took his place

on the runners, I jumped aboard and away we went down to the slough of the Unalakleet River and over to the river itself. I had just relaxed beneath the canvas sled cover, when the sound of crunching ice brought me very much to life. With one jump, I cleared the sled by four feet before Fred could explain it was overflow ice and nothing to fear. Pressure brought on by the extreme cold had caused the river ice to crack and water seeping through had refrozen in thin layers over the surface. I took my place again, but riding over transparent river ice always gave me an uncomfortably insecure sensation. The opaque salt water ice of the Bering Sea was much more safe in appearance.

The dogs lapsed into an even trot. When they slowed down, we would talk to them or clap our hands in encouragement, but for the most part they chose their own pace.

Our objective was to photograph pressure ice. Fred had set aside this winter to record in color movies the life of an Eskimo village from freeze-up in fall through the spring break-up. Weather phenomena of a Far Northern winter was one important phase. Since the wind had blown up to 50 miles per hour for several days past, there was a good chance some ice floes might have broken off the main Bering Sea ice field and in smashing back against it churned up some interesting ice formations.

We didn't have to go far to find what we were looking for. About seven miles down the coast, we could look seaward and make out an ice wall high as a three-story building. We chained the dogs to separate stumps and logs of driftwood, to prevent their fighting, and walked out.

The sea proved to be a capricious ice mason. Opalescent blocks the size of a concert piano were balanced and angled in fantastic disarrangement. The colors drawn from this jumbled mass by the low level Arctic sun were unbelievable. Each separate crystal reflected hues shading from delicate jade to the deep blue of a sea cavern. We shot film by the yard and still there was always a new design to be caught.

Cold weather photography involved a definite technique. Fur mitts could be removed but woolen undergloves were a necessity since, with one touch to metal, the hand would come away minus flesh. Fred's movie cameras were winterized, so he had no trouble, but I carried the large still camera inside my parka between takes to prevent the shutter from freezing. While we worked, we watched each other's faces for any telltale patches of white. If one began to appear, a simple warming with the bare hands took care of it.

About mid-afternoon we selected two comfortable-looking ice cakes and sat down for a luncheon of canned tongue, hard tack and tea. I remember Fred had just stood to point something out when suddenly the ice beneath us seemed to shift. A startled look came over his face. He reached for my arm as another violent and more prolonged tremor seized the ice wall. For a moment the whole world seemed to rock. We heard the sharp cracking split of ice and above that the more ominous murmur of open water. We were terrified. Without another thought for our meal we grabbed up our cameras and ran. Not until we were safe on land-locked ice did we look back to see the pressure ice wall become a writhing, cubed python.

Enormous boulders pushed up from underneath toppling the superstructure in a grinding crash. Compositions of incredible asymmetry emerged only to reform in another startling pattern with the next convulsive heave. Just as suddenly as it began, the spectacle stopped. For a moment, one solitary column continued to teeter uncertainly, then settled back and all was quiet.

There was no more picture-taking that day. Daylight was gone and we were too exhausted. Not only the fright of being caught in the forces of Nature but the impact of the beauty had proved overwhelming. We realized we had lived one of our most memorable moments completely alone in a desert of ice.

It turned out to be our only attendance upon the birth of pressure ice during our stay among the Eskimos. Although we were out on the ice field many times, the winds and changing tides coincided with our being on the spot just this once.

Back at the Trading Post, we were impatient to see the results of our photography, but first the cameras had to be warmed by degrees in an outer room to prevent fogging and moisture. This was a precaution we followed in reverse whenever we went out.

Processing our still film at the Trading Post required some improvisation. Only one factor remained constant and that was our dark room—no problem when total darkness descended by 4 p.m. Our solutions were another matter. Water had to be melted from ice and heated to just the correct temperature on our oil range. Negatives were rinsed in a series of mixing bowls and finally hung to dry by thumbtacks in the archway between the kitchen and front room. They were printed next night by the light of a gasoline lamp.

We mailed our movie film to the States to be developed. We took the precaution of splitting shipments, sending out half one week and half the next. But we were always in an agony until the film had completed its 10,000 mile trip and was back at the Trading Post for viewing with a flashlight swathed in tissue paper.

Mail day was like Christmas once a week. There was the final exciting rush to get letters in the mailbags before the 10 a.m. deadline, when Postmaster Ryan would hitch up his dogs and drive out to the air strip. This was the signal for the entire village to start crowding in downstairs. With mail order catalogues, unemployment and old age pension checks coming in regularly, there was a good chance for every family to find something in its box. Speculation over whether or not the plane would stop that particular day was always a topic of conversation, although only two regular runs were missed due to weather conditions the entire winter. With the arrival of the Postmaster downstairs, we declared a moratorium on our work. All of our mail was piled in the middle of the table and given complete attention until each letter had been read separately and together several times, each color slide studied and exclaimed over, each magazine and paper up to six weeks old perused.

With the arrival of the second mail plane after our marriage we were on hand to bid Uncle Charlie good-bye. He was leaving for a four months' vacation "outside," in the States. From then on, we took over management of the Trading Post. This meant maintaining a working schedule—a new experience for an artist and writer.

We had to be up and have breakfast eaten in time for the

opening of the store at eight-thirty and at the same time, there had to be a big pot of coffee ready for the clerks and "callers."

Eskimo women loved to call. They came for a variety of reasons. Some came out of curiosity, some asked advice but mostly they came because they liked small talk. They thoroughly enjoyed discussing their various aches in great detail. I didn't quite finish my cakes and coffee the day one proud mother described with graphic gestures the details of nursing a gangrenous leg.

Sinrock Mary was a frequent caller in our kitchen. Sinrock was known as "the Reindeer Queen of Alaska" because at one time she had owned over 50,000 reindeer. She had started her herds from a few head received for her services as an interpreter to U.S. officials who went to Siberia to purchase the first reindeer. The Reindeer Queen's herds had since dwindled to 500.

"Not like then," Sinrock would moan.

"I have lotsa deer. Everybody come to Sinrock. Now I old," she shook her head.

"No deer. Nobody come." Sinrock was indeed old. She herself didn't know her exact age, but the vertical tattooed lines on her chin showed she had been a young girl many years ago when this was considered an attractive decoration.

When she said "Nobody come" she was probably making a bid for sympathy, because she was well liked and respected by the entire village. Throughout her long life, she had adopted and cared for a number of orphaned children and it was with one of them she was making her home.

"Would you sell me some deer?" I asked.

Sinrock watched my face closely as I talked. When she had thought out what I was saying, she burst into moaning again,

"You take deer. I give you deer."

"No," I insisted, "we want to buy some."

"You take 'em. Traeger good to me. You take deer."

I caught on. "All right," I reached for the credit book. "I take deer. You take what you want in Trading Post." This was entirely agreeable.

At this point, our bargaining was interrupted by a piercing scream from below.

Fred came running out of the front room, "What was that?"

Before I could reply, we heard another scream followed by the sound of objects thudding against the walls.

Fred took the stairs in three leaps and landed in the middle of a raging battle between two of the village matrons. Oswald and Lowell had succeeded in pulling them apart, but not before some canned goods had been hurled and one wrist cut. The vanquished came upstairs to have a bandage put on.

"Does it hurt?" I inquired.

"No," she answered in gentle, ladylike tones.

I didn't ask what the trouble was and she didn't tell me.

Sinrock was simply transported with curiosity. While first aid was being given, she tapped her cane on the floor in a tune of agitation. As my patient stood up to leave, the Reindeer Queen made an abrupt departure to hobble after her.

Fred told me later, the ruckus arose out of a husband, wife, other woman triangle—eternal even in Eskimo land.

Wife met homebreaker. Wife hurled canned milk.

We thought this would be the end of the affair, but, just a few days later, wife herself came in with a watch to be sent off for repair. There had been another tussle in her home when the other woman came to apologize.

Wife won husband!

While I waylaid "callers" in the kitchen with a cup of coffee or a magazine, Fred was busy doing a series of native heads in pastel. This work, however, was frequently interrupted by trappers. Bringing in the heaviest load of mink, marten, fox, land otter and beaver was Pete Katungan.

"Hello," Fred greeted him, "looks like you did all right."

"I get my limit," Pete told him.

"You did! You must have been awfully busy."

"Yes," Peter agreed. Work was no novelty to him. He prepared for trapping season year round. All of his gear was kept in first class condition. His dog harnesses were always in repair, his sled was in good working order and his cache stocked with salmon to provide food for him and his team.

"How is it you always get your limit in before anyone else does?" Fred wanted to know.

"I go. I stay," the trapper declared with some feeling. "Some Eskimo he come, go alla time. Spend time on trail instead of trapping."

This was true. While many of the trappers were spending time going back and forth on frequent trips into the village, their unattended traps were robbed by wolves. But an even greater enemy of the trapper than the wolves was their native craving for sociability. As Pete summed up,

"Eskimo can't come back to his woman alla time and get limit."

Fred picked up one of the "blankets," the largest sized beaver pelts of greatest value.

"How much?"

Pete shrugged. Unless addressed directly, he stood by with seeming indifference while the skins were being examined. Fred called in the Eskimo clerks, Lowell and Oswald, to help him judge the skins. They noted the size and color, then examined it closely to see if there had been any damage from rubbing. Other pelts were given a deft shake to determine the thickness and quality of fur. They arrived at a price.

"All right?" Fred asked.

"Yeah."

Pete was given a slip crediting purchases in the amount of the value of the furs. Uncle Charlie's only profit was the normal markup on merchandise.

Most transactions weren't as simply handled as trading with Pete.

More often than not, the Eskimo trapper had to obtain credit before going out on trail, so his family could eat during his absence. In addition, he would charge his own grub-stake against anything he might bring back. Even though grubstaking trappers, prospectors and fishermen was a common practice among traders, it was not without problems, for unfortunately the needs of wives and children went on whether the trappers were successful or not. If a trapper returned empty-handed, Uncle Charlie always proved to be morally incapable of holding human welfare as collateral against the debt. He would "carry" the family and as his only hope of remuneration was the trapper, he would grubstake again. The result was thousands of dollars of unpaid accounts on his books, accounts which he eventually wrote off. This the Eskimos accepted as a matter of course. Perhaps the ancient idea of sharing and caring had something to do with it. They saw that Uncle Charlie was better off so they expected to receive from him. The number of hours he worked, the risks and responsibilities he assumed had nothing to do with it.

Since the extreme cold held for several weeks, we were unable to photograph any outdoor activities. The Eskimos stayed in their homes as much as they could—just emerging to saw enough wood to stoke the fire. We used to watch and marvel that wood wasn't stacked ahead of time so that this sub-zero activity might be eliminated.

Fred very much wanted to photograph an Eskimo family living in the old-time way before ancient customs entirely disappeared. For this sequence, he selected the family of his favorite trailmate and model, Achebuk.

Achebuk was a seal hunter, both fearless and cunning, but more to our interest were his photogenic qualities. He had a magnificent head with strong, high cheek bones and perfectly proportioned features. In contrast to a face of classic oriental inscrutability was a fun loving disposition and a natural bent toward play acting.

We asked our good friend the Commissioner, Stevan Ivanoff, to act as our interpreter since Mrs. Achebuk did not understand English at all and because even though Achebuk could speak a little, he had not mastered it to the extent of explaining what we wanted.

It soon became a game between Achebuk and Stevan to reproduce in setting and in actions as nearly as possible the way a family had lived when they were boys. Stevan made many trips from his home to the Achebuk cabin carrying ancient wooden platters, fish nets, spoons and skins.

We in turn, lugged camera equipment and the only gasoline motor in the village to provide power for lighting. Our two photofloods proved to be too much of a load but before realizing it, we had made five unsuccessful beginnings and burned out as many lamps. Added to that were the physical limitations of the little eight-by-eleven room which were severely strained with Achebuk, his wife and son and daughter, ourselves and camera equipment, Stevan and the noisy motor. In the middle of all the confusion, a neighbor woman came to call and shortly afterward, two children drifted in. We never learned why they came but they bobbed in and out during the entire goings on.

The scene started with the Achebuk family asleep in a bed of reindeer skins unrolled on the floor.

With convincing yawns and stretches, Achebuk arose to exit through a bearskin draped entryway to gather snow for morning water. This he placed in a kettle on a small Yukon stove of a type introduced to the Eskimos by prospectors at the turn of the century. Then he laid a fire from shavings prepared the night before—another trick the Eskimos learned

from the old Sourdoughs. Next, the family began stirring
and here Stevan, who had become the director as well as
interpreter and property man, interrupted the proceedings.

With wide gestures and vigorous head shaking he pointed
to Mrs. Achebuk. "Her hair not right. Not like old time Eskimo wear it."

Achebuk looked up from his acting and when Stevan explained in native what was wrong, directed a dark look
toward his wife for spoiling his scene.

"Ask her if she would please fix it in the old time way for
us," Fred told or rather shouted to Stevan, who had difficulty
hearing.

Stevan relayed the request to Achebuk who in turn yelled
it to Mrs. Achebuk because she was almost completely deaf.
Mrs. Achebuk obediently parted her hair in the center to
make a coiled loop behind each ear, which she bound with
strips of fur. Then we were ready to continue.

While the family pulled on their boots, Achebuk lit the
fire. In no time at all, the temperature soared to the 90's.
With perspiration streaming down everyone's face, our drama
of life in the frozen North continued. It was an example of
real showmanship and—a love of food—for the meal Stevan
had planned was an Eskimo banquet.

The first course was trout boiled with their heads on and
without seasoning. They were eaten from a common platter
on a traditional four-inch-high table around which the diners
squatted. Achebuk as head of the family was entitled to the
broth which he carried to his mouth in a large wooden spoon.
This was the only flatware in evidence, the more common
usage involving the first two fingers and thumb.

The second course was dried salmon dipped in seal oil followed by "quak"—fish which was frozen, then thawed and eaten raw.

And finally came the climax to this gastronomic orgy—"*A-koo-tuk*," the favorite of all native foods. To create it, Mrs. Achebuk had kneaded about a pound of reindeer tallow to a creamy consistency. To this she added a bit of water, a dash of seal oil and, as a final touch, berries—salmon berries, blueberries and low bush cranberries which had been stored in a keg since summer. When thoroughly mixed, it was ready for eating. How they loved it! There was no mistaking their relish for acting. Stevan watched the scene closely. His eyes were bright; he swallowed frequently. Before the *a-koo-tuk* was half eaten, he broke in to the scene.

"Nah! Nah! You eat wrong," he told one of the young-sters who was scooping the delicacy up by the handful. "Watch me," he held up just two fingers, then scraping around the bowl shoveled an egg-sized bite into his mouth. "That way," he instructed licking his lips. Like any good director, he continued to demonstrate the gesture until the end of the scene when all the *a-koo-tuk* was gone.

We ourselves tried a bite and found it surprisingly tasty. The tart berries cut the fat and the seal oil didn't approach the ranker cheeses enjoyed in the States.

When the photography was finally finished, it was evening. As we prepared to leave, Mrs. Achebuk stopped us to say something in Eskimo.

"She say for you come to Eskimo Woman's Sewing Club tomorrow," Stevan interpreted. Mrs. Achebuk spoke further. "She say for you both to come."

And so it came about we made our bow to Eskimo society the following day.

TOMCOD FISHER

CHAPTER III

ESKIMO PARTY

"IR-EE-GEE! (not good)" Miowak pointed to the patch of gauze on her foster son's neck. "What wrong?"

"Oh, just a little cut," Fred shrugged. "Say, there certainly is a big turnout today."

I was glad he changed the subject before anyone in the Sewing Club associated the bandage with my husband's new haircut. Unfortunately my first wielding of clippers and scissors had also been a letting of blood. Even more distressing was the haircut itself which strongly suggested a wheatfield in a windstorm.

Several of the members made room for us on the floor.

They were all very busy making clothes for the village poor. Some of the women hand-stitched parka coverings while others worked on Eskimo boots called "mukluks."

Mukluks, in addition to being beautiful examples of native handicraft, were extremely practical footgear.. The reindeer-skin tops were warm yet light in weight. The durable soles of giant seal skin remained waterproof over a period of hours.

For extreme, dry cold, there were boots with fur soles sewed in opposite directions to prevent skidding. This style,

brought over by the Lapp reindeer herders, was the ultimate in cold weather comfort. Yet, many of the seamstresses preferred to sell their lovely mukluks in order to purchase shiny black rubber boots such as the white man wore—for lack of anything better, and wholly unsuited to a Northern winter.

I sat beside Stevan's daughter, Emily, who had been "outside" to school. In her speaking she gave an impression of sophistication.

"How is the new Mrs. Machetanz today?"

"Fine," I replied, "How are you?"

"Very well, thank you." There was a pause.

"Did you see the Northern Lights last night?" I asked.

"Yes."

Here her mother who had been listening closely interrupted, "It mean a change in weather."

"It does? I hope so. When it gets warm enough we're going on our honeymoon to St. Michael's."

"*Ah-ree-gah!*" the mother said. "You go with dog team?"
I nodded.

"You like to drive dogs?" Emily sounded incredulous.

"Oh yes," I answered positively. "In fact, I'll probably do all the driving."

Their blank looks told me my attempt at humor had misfired, still I enjoyed a laugh with myself at the very thought of Fred lolling in the sled while I took over the dogs.

This was my first insight into Eskimo literalism. My second came shortly.

"We had a nice time. You must come and see us," Fred said upon leaving.

"We come," our hostess replied and they did—the very next week. Over fifty women filed into the Trading Post for one of the largest meetings on record.

After this flurry of social activity, our life resettled into a pattern.

Fred devoted his mornings to painting and I to "callers." During the afternoons, there was Trading Post business but we always tried to spent part of the time scouting picture possibilities. Frequently we took the dogs on a run so they would be in shape for longer trips once the cold broke. Evenings more often than not brought over-night guests.

At this time of year, our guests were mostly "bush pilots," a distinct breed of Alaskan adventurer. Some maintained regular mail and passenger runs between villages, others were air-borne traders and a few experimented with showing movies wherever an electric generator made it possible. This manner of commerce had made airplanes almost as commonplace in Eskimo country as automobiles were in the States.

Far from being limited, our larder afforded quite a varied menu for our boarders. We had every type of canned goods including crab and hams and there was fresh salmon trout caught in traps under the ice of the Unalakleet River. We had barbecued ribs and deerburger from Sinrock Mary's reindeer. Uncle Charlie's stock of "shipped in" frozen fowls were frequently supplemented with delectable quail-like ptarmigan brought in by hunters.

With all our activities, days slipped into weeks and it was time for another haircut.

Fred had just braced himself in our improvised barber chair one Sunday morning when Lowell burst into the room, "Eula's house is on fire!"

FIRE! No more dreaded word was ever spoken in the Far North.

With one motion, Fred was off the chair and grabbing a load of fire extinguishers Uncle Charlie always kept at hand.

"Get CAA," he called over his shoulder as he ran after Lowell.

I rushed to our phone connecting with the air strip, "Fire at Eula's."

The click at the other end told me the message was understood and that help would be coming to the village shortly.

I grabbed my parka (it was still 35° below) and an armful of extinguishers and hurried to Eula's where scores of Eskimos were milling around.

It turned out to be no more than a chimney fire, which was quickly extinguished, but no matter how small, fire was taken very seriously. All of the buildings in the village were of log or clapboard and with the usual steady wind blowing, there was never much hope of stopping the flames once they were under way.

We came back to the Trading Post and packed the extinguishers to be sent to the factory for refueling and then we took a long look at the hazard we were running.

All of our fifteen thousand feet of exposed and unexposed film were in our room, plus thousands of still film. Our movie cameras, our enlarger, a book manuscript, our correspondence, everything that was of value to us was in a room with an oil burning stove, next to the kitchen where the range burned day and night. The room was over wood burning stoves in the basement and on the first floor. To be sure, the Trading Post exterior was corrugated iron, but underneath were logs.

Before the day was over, we had drawn up a priority list of things to go first in the event of fire.

We placed our movie film in a trunk by one of the front room windows easily accessible from a snowbank outside. A special bag with a long rope was made for the cameras so they could be lowered from our bedroom window. Our correspondence, the Trading Post books and the manuscript were placed in labeled boxes next to the window and finally we went through several fire drills with the Eskimo clerks, Lowell and Oswald. Then we breathed more freely but we were never away from the Post any length of time that we didn't utter a prayer of relief at our first glimpse of that big barn-like structure we called "home."

Our various stoves posed problems other than fire.

There was the eternal question of fuel. Wood had to be hauled in from the forests three miles behind Unalakleet or gathered from driftwood scattered along the beach. Our oil stoves were more convenient but feed pipes remained subject to freezing if the least amount of water condensed during changes in temperature.

The big kitchen range introduced yet another element of chance whenever it was used for cooking. Somehow during the process of converting it from a wood burner, all of the heat had been channeled to the top. In order to turn out a cake for Fred's birthday party in late February, it was necessary to shove into the oven, in order, one inverted pie tin upon which sat the cake covered with a dish rack supporting a chopping block and two pans of cold water.

Our refreshments for the party also included ice cream, that being one of the favorite dishes of the Eskimos. Since neither of us had previously operated hand freezers, we made the mistake of waiting until too late to start the process. As a result Fred ate his dinner with one hand and cranked with the other while I ate mine standing on top of the bucket, because one of the clasps was broken.

Our party was to start at eight o'clock. At seven-thirty, there was a knock on the door.

It was Stevan and his wife resplendent in their "dress" parkas. Mrs. Ivanoff's was made of reindeer skin fringed with wolverine around the hem and upper arm. Stevan's was ground squirrel, beautifully pieced together and trimmed with a three inch wide border of intricate design. What distinguished both the parkas and put them in the category of "dress-up" clothes were the wolverine strips hanging from the upper part both front and back. These were more than a decoration. They were a mark of the high born—of those

descended from illustrious forebears. At the same time, they were an evidence of class distinction in the village. I once asked Stevan why anybody couldn't decorate a parka with them and thus join the elite. "But they would be laughed at," was the reply and his tone told me nothing could be more humiliating.

By ten minutes to eight, all our dozen Eskimo guests had arrived.

Mrs. Ivanoff made us a present of an "ooloo," a semi-circular bladed knife with a stone handle. It was used largely in woman's work; to clean fish and sew and cut skins. Miowak brought a long bone needle. One of the finest presents was a large wooden bowl.

"We had one like it once," Postmaster Frank Ryan announced. "All the men used to carry wooden bowls when the village celebrated the first snowfall."

"What did they use them for?" Fred asked.

"It was part of the celebration," Frank settled himself to

reminisce. "When the first snow fell, all the men would go to the Kashim. They would paint themselves along here," he indicated his ribs, "and across the eyebrows and face. Then they would sing and dance around the Kaskim faster and faster and finally the Chief would lead them all out into the village, everybody yelling. At the time of the first snowfall, no one left the village. Everyone was home but the men at the Kashim. When the men left the Kashim, each one carried a wooden bowl. They went to every house. The leader would back through the door but the others walked straight in. My mother would fill the dishes with food, with berries and fish. It was a good time for the men but when I was little and they came to our house, I was so scared I hid under skins so they couldn't see me."

Frank's recollection started off an evening of storytelling.

Another guest remembered the time his grandfather had been chosen to accept a Potlatch invitation from a neighboring village. The invitation had come in the form of a wooden stick upon which were carved signs representing the names of those invited. It was his grandfather's coveted task to carry back a stick bearing signs of the families accepting. By cunning and stealth, the messenger managed to slip into the Kashim of the host village without being seen, a feat which brought great honor to Unalakleet.

There were tall tales of mighty medicine men who allowed a walrus tusk to be drawn completely through their bodies and lived to tell about it and there were stories of the Little Men—midgets who roamed the tundra and fulfilled the role of gremlin for the Eskimo. Although Christianity had come to the village and chiefs and medicine men no longer pro-

duced strange magic, stories of their exploits were still related a little nervously and listened to with solemn atten-
tiveness.

The evening became one of eerie unreality, a mood en-
hanced by grotesque shadows from the flickering lamp. Then
Frank told of how the Kashim shook the day the Old
Chief died and when he ended the story unexpectedly with a
leap into the air and a savage "Yih!," everyone including
the host and hostess jumped as if the Old Chief himself had
suddenly materialized. There were even those among us who
would have sworn the Trading Post shook.

The party ended around ten o'clock.

We followed our guests to the outside door where they repeated their *"Coo-yah-hahs"* (thank yous). The night air was
noticeably warmer.

"It turning into Lady Winter," Achebuk observed.

"Oh I hope not." We still had quite a few winter activities
to film.

"Better not talk against Nature. When you need good
weather, spirits won't help."

But the "spirits" must not have heard me, for our false
spring was short lived. Overnight the thermometer dropped
50 degrees, to 20° below. When this happened, the Eskimos
asserted that "The weather was working for someone," mean-
ing a victim. Fred and I were quite happy, however, now
that we could follow our photographic schedule. But the work
we counted on doing in March was frequently interrupted
by salesmen arriving to take next year's orders. They were
like messengers from another world and we thoroughly enjoyed their visits. The salesmen, in turn, were pleased to find

southern fried chicken being served on the shores of the
Bering Sea.

I started taking lessons in the Eskimo language. Three
dialects were spoken in the village. Malemute was the one
most widely used throughout the North Country, so my efforts
were concentrated on it.

My teacher was silver-haired David Panipchuk. He was
one of Fred's favorite models because he not only held a pose
well, but regaled the artist with amusing stories.

He had seen more of Alaska than most of the older Eskimos having been a cook on a Yukon River boat during the
Gold Rush. He knew enough of life "outside" to want to see
a circus more than anything else in the world. He used to ask
me to tell him of circuses, of each of the acts in detail. When
I described acrobatics, Dave wasn't impressed. The Eskimos
had their own brand of physical feats of skill.

"My father, he strong and quick. Once at the games at St.
Michael's, he turn over in his kayak nine times. He win
prize."

This meant Dave's father had made nine complete turns
going under water and coming up again without sinking his
skin boat. The average kayaker might expect to turn over as
many as three times without filling his boat more than half
full of water, which would still allow him to stay afloat.

There was no written language among the Eskimos. Dave
helped me to compose a phonetic one. To my surprise, I found
moods and tenses and numbers to correspond to the English
language. But it was slow work. My lessons required a great
deal of studying, about which Dave used to tease me. Once
when he caught me poring over my notes, he shook his head,

"White man sit and read. Eskimo he sit and think." Then he grinned, "Better not read too hard. Thinking too much give Eskimo headache. Maybe you the same."

Just then, Lowell came in, his face shining, "I got boy! I got boy!"

"Congratulations, Lowell. Now you have another hunter in the family." I turned to Oswald who happened to be in the kitchen trimming wicks on the gasoline lamps. "Isn't that wonderful?"

"Yeah," Oz answered without bothering to glance up from his work.

Dave saw my look of surprise and laughed.

"Oswald too lucky. He have boys—four. His woman want girl so bad she pretend little boy is girl and won't cut his hair."

The next day I went calling on Mrs. Anagik and her new son. She told me that her own grandmother, Miowak, had attended the birth. This wasn't Miowak's regular line of work, however. The official village midwife was Thora Katchatag, who had been trained by a nurse and had up to a hundred successful deliveries to her credit.

Since the new mother was still tired, I did not stay long but the bright winter sunshine tempted me to walk farther. I decided to drop in on grandmother Miowak to offer my congratulations for both the delivery and the new grandson.

"*Yah! Yah!* Come in," Miowak greeted me with her almost toothless grin. Like many of the older women in the village, she had worn her teeth almost to the gums working oogruk skin for boot soles. "I fix *kupiak* (coffee)."

We sipped our *kupiak* and Miowak recounted the doings

of her several adopted children, who crawled over our feet and burrowed into our laps. This happy air of confusion was increased when Great-grandmother came in with a sack of tomcod. She had been down at the river mouth all afternoon fishing through a hole in the ice. Providing tomcod for the family and dogs was a job delegated strictly to the older women.

Now she opened the sack to show us her catch.

"*Ah-ree-gah!*" Miowak's eyes sparkled.

"How will you cook them?" I asked her.

"Oh, I boil them. What we don't eat, I freeze—"

Here Great-grandmother interrupted in voluble Eskimo. Miowak interpreted. "She say that not the best way. She like to keep tomcod in warm place two, three days then put in cache. No wind get them, they freeze. Wait a long time, month maybe, then cut belly open, eat liver first. Take off skin, eat sides."

"Oh? You mean eat them just as they come from the cache?"

Miowak shook her head, "No, thaw first. She think tomcod best if left in cache through winter and thaw when weather thaw. But," Miowak added, "nobody eat them that way anymore. They too strong. Have to eat them with long teeth." This I took correctly to mean she could hardly bring herself to bite into them.

Through her daughter, Great-grandmother promised to fix some tomcod and give me a taste. She further stated she would save the backbone just for me.

"That special part," Miowak explained. "Shhhh!" she turned to one of the children who had started crying, "I take you out in snow and leave you. No clothes on, too."

The child continued to cry.

"Shhhh!" Great-grandmother commanded, following it up with several words in her own language. Miowak laughed. "She say she make baby chew salmon eggs. Stick lips together."

The child quieted.

"Nashalik get seal this morning. I see him pull it on his sled," Miowak confided.

"He did? Where?"

"Out at edge of ice. More seal come soon. I promise your *Weegah* I make seal poke so he take pictures!"

"*Weegah* means Fred?"

"*Weegah* means 'beloved husband,' " she grinned knowingly, "you tell him I ready soon."

"Thanks, Miowak, I will tell my '*Weegah.*' I must go now. I have a lot of work to do."

"*Bee-rah-in,*" Miowak and her mother waved good-bye.

"*Bee-rah-itic,*" I called back. I had spent much more time

than I should have visiting when Fred and I were planning a trip the next day with Kootuk to his fish trap. Kootuk had told us this would be a good time because a recent storm had caused the fish to become active in the river, thereby increasing his chances of a big haul.

While Fred assembled camera equipment, I tried to figure out food for the three of us for three days as I packed our extra boots, underclothes and socks.

The next morning, we added dog chains and a bundle of dried salmon to the loaded sled and set out following Kootuk at about an eighth of a mile. It was another perfect winter day with pure blue skies above us and beneath us a trail made fast by recent snow. A taut tow-line assured us our dogs were all pulling well.

Soon we began to see trees, chiefly spruce with some cottonwood and birch. I hadn't realized how much I had missed them until we left the tripod trail markers of the tundra to enter the forests. These were the trees that enabled the Eskimos of Unalakleet to build log cabins instead of the sod and driftwood huts of the natives farther north, where the land was barren.

We arrived at Kootuk's one room cabin in late afternoon. While I prepared dinner, Fred and Kootuk chained the dogs out, fed them a dried salmon apiece, gathered water from a hole chopped through the river ice, and split wood. Darkness came on quickly. At dinner, we lit a candle and crouched around a wooden crate, barely able to make out what we were eating. There was no chit-chat. Eating was a serious business to Kootuk and he gave it his undivided attention.

But once the meal was finished, he discoursed at length

upon fish and fishing. He knew that he would have a good chance of catching salmon trout because they would come upstream with the warmer weather. Grayling there would be, because grayling stayed in the river all the time. The lush traveled back and forth going down to feed on tomcod at the river mouth. He told us he set his traps under the ice in winter because the fish all left the river at break-up but with the fall they returned once more. He pointed out that fish in winter would not take a hook or eat anything and that they all had ice in their stomachs.

Fred and I sat listening expectantly for the next bit of lore. All at once a wild, unearthly howl sounded so close that even Kootuk gave a start.

"What was that?" I asked in terror.

"Wolf," Kootuk had regained his composure, but by this time the team was howling in chorus. "Dogs scare him away. They don't like wolf."

"I thought some of the dogs were bred to wolves, Kootuk," Fred paused in dividing a skillet of bacon grease between the three of us.

"*Naga,*" Kootuk shook his head. "Sometimes female crossed with male but it not make good dog. Lean face. Tail hang down. Dog with wolf blood tire in spring. No good."

Kootuk swiped at his share of bacon grease with a piece of bread as we all did. The grease just hit the spot after traveling all day in the cold.

Next morning we headed for Kootuk's fish traps a few miles up-river. This site was his by right of inheritance and no other Eskimo would think of poaching.

Kootuk cut and shoveled his way to the two wire cylinders

set one on top, the other beneath the ice. He had been following the same procedure twice a month from the time they were installed, so the ice here was only six inches thick. Elsewhere on the river, it was four feet. A fence strung from each bank completely blocked the river except for funnel openings into the traps.

Kootuk tugged and pulled the first cylinder on to the ice where he emptied its squirming contents while we watched in amazement. There was over 100 pounds of salmon, lush and grayling. And the other trap yielded an equal amount! We were elated, both for Kootuk's good fortune and for the photographic subject matter. We exclaimed at length but the only evidence of Kootuk's pleasure was the tune he hummed over and over while he worked.

Once the haul had been loaded into his sled and the traps reset, we started back to the cabin. Upon breaking out of the forest, we were surprised to find a wind had come up, obliterating the tracks left by Kootuk, who was by now out of sight.

To make matters worse, we were in open country and there were no familiar landmarks to show us the way. The wind increased, enveloping us in a cloud of swirling, stinging snow. We rode for what seemed much longer than we should have and still no sled tracks appeared to guide us.

Fred became concerned. He had been lost on trail before and had endured a 40° below night with only a sled cover for protection. His face had frozen so badly on that occasion, it was months healing. Naturally he had little desire for us to repeat the experience.

Although I was covered by a tarpaulin and comfortable

enough, Fred was forced to ride the runners to watch for the cut off. He shielded his face to keep his eyelashes from freezing together and gave the dogs free rein. And so we went along for another hour.

Suddenly in the middle of a vast snow-covered plain with no sign of a trail, Blackie veered sharply to the right across country and in a short time brought us to Kootuk's cabin. Like any good leader, he had stuck to the scent of the dog team he had been following. Now, I could fully appreciate the adage, "A man's life out on trail is no better than the integrity of his lead dog."

We feasted on salmon trout that night. It was a real delicacy which we ate with especial relish because we were all together again in a snug, warm cabin.

The next morning, the wind having abated, we returned to Unalakleet. Except for some anxious moments during the storm, it had been a good trip.

We had obtained rare pictures of a craft that was no longer being pursued among the Eskimos. As for Kootuk, he had timed his catch well. The Trading Post would buy his fish at a premium price of 25 cents per pound in trade because there would be a ready market. The next few days would bring many visitors to Unalakleet to attend the annual Swedish Lutheran Church Conference schedule to start within the week.

ESKIMO DANCE AND DRUMMER

Chapter IV

DOG SLED HONEYMOON

"Five more dog teams come from shaktoolik," Daisy, my dishwasher confided. With Stevan on vacation, Daisy came after school each day to help do housework. Although she was only twelve years old, her ear for news was quite as sharp as her eye for dust. "Frank have three dog teams at his house," she continued. This meant three visiting families. Dogs required a sizable amount of dried salmon and the supply that year had been small. Since it was easier to feed humans than dogs, emphasis was placed accordingly.

Here her recital was interrupted by a loud stamping at the head of the steps. It was Achebuk.

"Machetanz here?"

"No he isn't, Ach. He's helping Frank sort the mail. Is there anything I can do?"

"Achebuk need food. More families come to stay last night."

"Oh no! Don't they know you already have more than you can handle? Can't you ask them to stay with someone else?"

Achebuk shrugged. "No. They stay anywhere they want unless somebody sick there. Used to be Chief asked visitors to go to homes with most fish. Now no Chief."

"My father give away whole bundle of fish and seal oil," Daisy told us proudly.

Achebuk sighed. "Winter divide the Eskimos. It show rich and poor. Not like summer. Everybody the same then."

But hardships like Achebuk's resulting from the Church Conference were more than offset for the Eskimos by the benefits.

The Conference provided an excellent excuse for visiting which might not otherwise have taken place. Families came from miles around, the oldsters to reminisce, the young marrieds to compare progeny and the maids and youths to form acquaintances, a good many of which later ended in marriage.

In addition, public gatherings were held as often as three times a day. There were sermons with Panipchuk interpreting into native, sentence by sentence, and there was a choir and much singing to satisfy the Eskimo love for music. To the edification of all concerned, a substantial number of conversions took place, for the Eskimos were quick to admit wrongs and anxious to do better. These confessions remained topics of conversation for weeks to come.

Daisy referred to one now. "A lady tell how she chase her husband out of the house with stove wood last night."

"Who?" Achebuk sat up, his economic difficulties forgotten.

"Oh she not from here," Daisy teased.

Just then Fred came in and dumped our mail on the table. "Hello, Ach, how are you?"

"Need food. Stomach empty," Achebuk rubbed his middle for emphasis. Then he repeated his story of more visitors.

Fred thought it over. "Tell you what I'll do. We want to get pictures of seal hunting. You get what food you need at the Post. I'll pay your bill and you take us on a hunt. Okay?"

"Okay." Achebuk was happy again.

"When do you think would be the best time to go?"

"Can get seal now but better wait till little later," Achebuk advised. "Seal fatter then. Not sink so quick when shot."

"Good. We're taking our honeymoon to St. Michael soon. Maybe when we get back would be all right?"

"That all right."

"You'll have equipment, won't you?"

Achebuk reflected. "I need white parka cover. Seal see this, he get scared," he indicated his brown reindeer parka. "Wear white parka, seal think me ice."

"We'll have one made for you," Fred promised.

"Should wear it a little first. Get it dirty like spring ice."

"All right. We'll have it made in time for you to wear before we go. Do you have everything else you'll need?"

"I have harpoon and rifle. We use your sled and dogs but—" Achebuk became downcast again, "no kayak. You buy me oogruk skins, I make kayak."

"I can't do that, Ach. I can't afford it."

Now Achebuk was miserable. He rose to his feet and raised his face skyward. "Nobody love Achebuk," he lamented loudly.

We were dumbfounded. The last thing we had expected from this noble hunter was a show of emotion. But Achebuk knew us well and he was a born dramatizer of any situation.

Fred recovered first, "Maybe we can borrow one," he proposed. "But I don't want a kayak made out of canvas. I want an old-time one made out of skin. Do you know who might have one?"

Achebuk thought it over. He could think of no one in Una-lakleet but he knew of a hunter several miles north of the village who owned a kayak made out of skin. He would borrow that one.

"Then we're set." Fred was getting anxious to read our mail. "Okay?"

"Okay," Achebuk agreed and taking his leave hurried downstairs to buy his groceries, with Daisy close on his heels to collect her family's mail.

We turned to the heap of letters and newspapers and all was quiet, but only for a few minutes. There was an agonized howl from Fred, "Look at that!" He handed me the Nome paper.

On the front page was the story of our marriage and there in black-and-white for all to see was written that Mr. and Mrs. Machetanz were planning a honeymoon to St. Michael and *Mrs.* Machetanz would drive the dogs!

"Where in the world do you suppose they got that idea?" Fred asked.

Slowly a memory rose up. My "I don't know" changed to a question. "Does Emily Ivanoff write for the Nome paper?"

"Yes, she's their correspondent."

"Then I know where it came from," I admitted. "Me."

I told him of seeing Emily at the Eskimo Woman's Sewing Club and joking about doing all the driving.

"I'm afraid your joke turned out to be a joke on us," Fred commented wryly. And it had. Our friends who read the Nome paper didn't let us forget that one for a long time.

We began to make plans for our long anticipated honey-moon. In the midst of preparations we learned that Stevan, his wife and twelve-year-old grandson were also taking a trip to St. Michaels to visit relatives there. We suggested joining forces and were delighted when the idea proved acceptable to them. We knew Stevan would pick the best and safest route and that he and his wife would be excellent company. Mrs. Ivanoff's quiet indulgence was a perfect backboard for her husband's bouncing exuberance. While he spoke animatedly and at length, she sat silently by encouraging him with smiling attention and approving nods. But in the company of others, Mrs. Ivanoff was quite capable of spinning a few yarns of her own. We looked forward to the stories we hoped to hear fully as much as the travel itself. Everything was all set for departure within the week. Then I walked into the bedroom one afternoon and found Fred in bed with a temperature of 102°.

I rushed for the nurse, only to find she had gone to another village that morning. With a feeling of panic, I realized there was no other person to turn to. The nearest doctor was 150 air miles away in Nome. I went back to the Post and sat helplessly by as Fred's temperature continued to rise, now and again broken by violent chills. All through a night made long by worry, I watched for some improvement but there was none. By morning, I finally faced the possibility of pneumonia and decided something had to be done. Not knowing any specific treatment, my only recourse was to try every nursing procedure I'd heard of on the theory one at least might prove helpful. In the ensuing days I managed to interrupt my patient's sleep with continual temperature-taking and his daytime rest with bed making. I chilled him with baths and alcohol rubs and burned him with hot water bottles. Otherwise nutritious and tasty foods I ruined with overcooking and straining. Whichever one of the treatments was effective, if any, we never knew. Fred began to mend and nothing could keep him in bed after five days. Upon rising, in fact, he declared I would have killed him had he remained a patient any longer.

Two days later, we left for St. Michael on our honeymoon with Stevan's team leading the way. Since Fred was still weak from his illness, I did most of the dog driving *just as the Nome paper had said I would!*

We cut down to the beach, threaded our way for a time among inshore pressure ice and finally turned out to the Bering Sea ice field. Here the surface was smooth as a skating rink. We started out at a fast clip but before going very far, we were delayed by Stevan's team.

Stevan was trying to break in a new leader. This meant running alongside the dog and pointing the way whenever a change of direction was shouted. What baffled us was that the dog, instead of continuing the way Stevan pointed, would invariably wheel around and follow his master to the back of the sled, dragging the whole team behind him. It was a frustrating and wearing day for a man in his seventies.

We were not surprised to find him still resting in his sled when our team pulled into the seal-hunter's camp where we had all agreed to spend the night. With great effort, he rose to chain out his dogs. As he walked away, I noticed the wolverine strips trimming the back of his parka were knotted around something.

"What's that tied in your strips, Stevan?"

"Wha—What?" Stevan clawed at his back just as surprised and curious as I. "Here, here help me," he turned to Mrs. Ivanoff who was eying the situation, arms crossed, hands in sleeves.

In a few seconds she untangled the fur strips and as she did so several pieces of dried salmon fell to the ground.

Stevan began to understand. "You do that? You do that?" he demanded. Mrs. Ivanoff looked down hardly suppressing a smile while their grandson almost fell to the ground he was laughing so hard.

"What's the joke?" Fred looked up from staking the dogs.

"She tie salmon in my strips. That why the dogs follow me instead of go ahead all day," Stevan explained in exasperation.

We burst out laughing in spite of ourselves. Soon the whole camp was enjoying the story. By bedtime even Stevan was able to add a feeble chuckle to the general guffaws.

The half-dozen campers were in high spirits anyway. Hunting had been good, with three seals and four oogruk (giant seals) brought in that day. Seals were lying everywhere except within reach of the dogs. They would be taken home for the women to dress. From them would come blubber and fresh seal oil, flipper soup and skins for boots and parkas. Even the intestines would be used to make waterproof rain-parkas. For the Eskimos, spring hunting time was harvest time and the spirit of plenty and well being filled the camp. But there was no celebrating or late hours, for getting enough seal to last through the year was of grave importance and a hunter must have his rest. The camp quieted early.

Our party retired to one of the tents owned by a hunter who had returned to the village for the night. At the rear was a pile of dried grass with logs at the head and foot to form a crude bed which was unfortunately drawn up to Eskimo specifications and about ten inches too short for Fred and myself. Since we could not double up our legs with Mr. and Mrs. Ivanoff and their grandson also occupying the bed, there was nothing to do but dangle our feet over the end log all night. This alone would have made sleep improbable but it was made entirely impossible by the coming and going of seal hunters during the early morning hours. With each arrival and departure, all of the dogs in camp would set up a terrific din. So went the first night of our honeymoon.

We were glad when Stevan arose to build a fire in the half-oil-drum stove he had brought along. While Fred helped him with breakfast, Mrs. Ivanoff and I went for a walk on the tundra. I was sleepy but she seemed completely rested and ready for the trip ahead.

"My, you seem lively this morning," I told her. "I'm not quite awake yet."

"It easy for me to wake up. My grandmother teach me. When little girl, she get me up, dress me, take me out before sun come up. Then she bring me back and put me to bed. I learn to wake and get up early."

"Well, that's something I wish I'd learned."

Without bending her knees, Mrs. Ivanoff leaned over to gather a piece of moss. "This good for sore. Crumble it up and put on. It take the hurt away." Now she poked around for last year's blueberries in the brown patches of tundra blown free of snow. "Once we see bear. We stand still and watch him go way. I call bear bad name. My grandmother say 'Be quiet. He hear you. He know everything you say. Bear smart.' "

"Oh?" We started walking along the snow-covered beach.

Mrs. Ivanoff nodded. "One time long ago bear kill white man. Eskimo go kill bear. Chief say to bear 'Because you kill white man, you rot with him.' Then Eskimo wrap bear skin around white man." She gave me a sidelong look.

"Then what happened?"

"Leave bundle out all night before put in burial place. Next morning, white man get up and out of bear skin—"

"You don't mean it!"

"That right. Bear not want to rot with man so he bring him back to life."

We walked along while I thought this over. Mrs. Ivanoff told her stories with such a straight face, I never knew whether she believed them herself or was just having fun at my expense.

Now she glanced around and lowered her voice. "Once my grandmother see tracks of Little Men."

"She did?"

"That right." Mrs. Ivanoff turned her fist thumb up and pounded it into the snow. "The—track—look—like—this—" she paused after each word to make a dot across the top of the imprint.

I looked. There in the snow was a perfect miniature footprint!

We returned to the tent for breakfast after which Fred and I went to hitch our team. One glimpse of their harnesses and the dogs went wild with excitement—rolling in the snow, leaping and barking at each other and at the world. We felt the same urge to hit the trail. We would never have smoother, faster mushing nor more perfect weather. The skies remained a vibrant blue, the temperature a bracing 20° and the air pure energy to breathe. Today, with Stevan's dogs going ahead instead of trailing after him, we made much better time. By about three o'clock we had arrived at Herb Johnson's. He was the trader in St. Michael.

While we gorged on a dinner of reindeer stew prepared by his wife, Nelle, questions flew back and forth. The goings on in our respective villages held as much interest for us as a Sunday edition of a metropolitan newspaper. Herb knew most of the people we mentioned. Though thirty odd years younger than Uncle Charlie, he had lived over half his life in the North Country. He hated, loved and cussed his adopted land by turns but there was no getting away from it for he had become a part of it. Nelle, a vivacious and gregarious red-head, missed the sociability of city life. While Herb worked at the Post or turned out expertly carved ivory pieces in his spare time, she concentrated on making a "stateside" home. With white ruffled curtains and hand-crocheted runners she succeeded in imposing a real feeling of suburbia on the bleak shores of the Bering Sea.

Herb and Nelle's village could boast of a colorful past for St. Michael had been a center of trade as far back as the days of Russian Alaska. The influence of that early occupation in fact, was still to be seen in a picturesque Russian Church where services were held occasionally by a visiting priest. At the turn of the century, St. Michael had again prospered as a port for prospectors to change from ocean-going ships to stern-wheelers plying the Yukon River run to Dawson. Over 25,000 people had bustled along its board walks and regiments of soldiers had peopled its two-story barracks. Now the barracks and the walks were fallen in, the river boats were mere hulks along the beach and all that remained were the homes of about a hundred Eskimos.

But St. Michael was still a lively village. The second night we were there, the residents put on a dance which proved it.

By the time we arrived, the school room where the dance took place appeared to be packed with every man, woman and child in the village. The tittering of young girls, crooning to babies and deeper pitched laughs of the hunters made the room a solid block of sound. But once the drummers took their places on a bench facing a small cleared area, everyone grew quiet and waited. An older man wearing fur boots, parka and white cotton work gloves stepped into the center of the ring and the band struck up a tune. Their instruments, a hoop over which seal stomach had been stretched, were held erect by a small handle and beaten on the rim with a flexible stick, never on the skin. While drumming, the musicians chanted rhythmically and in unison in a singularly limited pitch.

The dance began, bizarrely spotlighted by a single glaring light-bulb. It was a series of powerful stamps, or flexing biceps and doubled fists with every sharp muscular movement proclaiming the power and joy of primitive strength. Soon the rhythm of the chanting drummers began to have its effect. As each dancer vied to outdo the other, in uninhibited contortions, the audience threw aside all restraint and encouraged the performers with wild applause and loud yells. Parkas were removed and finally shirts, but never the white cotton gloves worn by the male dancers. Then it was the women's turn. They usually danced in a group led by a man. One of the dances telling the story of a boat trip in a storm was performed while the women were seated on a bench. In contrast to the short and violent motions of the men, the women's gestures were long and graceful. Bracelets of reindeer hair held in the hands made each movement more sweeping.

And finally the children who were just learning the motions tried their skill. By the time everyone had had his chance, it was after eleven.

We stepped into the night to find the weather changed. A fine sleet stung our faces and in the lingering twilight we could make out great, billowing, dark clouds. All the next day, the storm continued and when finally we did wave good-bye to Herb and Nelle, it was under leaden skies.

The ice field was crisscrossed with cracks but Stevan, after a careful study of its condition, assured us travel would be quite safe as long as the strong inshore wind continued. On the return trip, we led the way—a situation which should have pleased our dogs—but they hated the wind and with tails tucked underneath their bodies and lowered heads, they plodded forward and took no joy in the trail.

Our weather cleared the second day out but the storm had left its mark. At a place called Tolstoi Point we found the ice field gone to sea, leaving a large expanse of open water. This provided a first look at the Bering Sea since freeze-up for our initial glimpse but what thrilled us even more was the exquisite blending of blues in the sea, the sky, the ice and snow. Blue-white icebergs of all shapes and sizes made islands in the deeper blue water, reflecting the morning sunshine like revolving mirrored balls. Above all was a sound we had almost forgotten—the soft lap of water filling the all-pervading blue-white hush.

"How would you like to build our home here some day?" Fred asked.

"It would be wonderful." In my mind I could see this fairyland of ice in the dawn.

But Fred had reconsidered. "You know the beauty here is only seasonal. When the ice is gone, there wouldn't be anything—not even trees."

"And it's slightly inaccessible," I was sobering too.

We turned our thoughts to getting past the point. Going inland was made impossible by a sheer bluff 80 feet high. Along its base on the beach, sections of ice lay piled like the ruins of an ancient city. On the outer edges of this white rubble was a mantle overhanging the water and narrowing to 30 inches in places. This was the route we chose to take.

I edged ahead holding a chain attached to the bow of the sled for a guide line. Then came the dogs, instinctively hugging the ledge. Finally came Fred, taking most of the weight at the back of the sled. We were so absorbed in the operation we'd no idea anyone was near by, but once around, we found Pete Katungan had been an interested spectator. Now he called to Fred from atop some piled up ice.

"Your wife good as Eskimo woman."

This was the highest praise he could have given me and I felt deeply flattered.

Fred stopped our team. "Hi, Pete, what are you doing here?"

"Hunting seal." Pete scrambled down to visit with us while we waited for Stevan to round the point. "I see gulls this morning. Spring come now sure."

How right Pete's prediction was we soon found out, for spring coincided with our arrival back in Unalakleet.

Overnight, the air changed from a tingling smack to a soft caress. In the village square and between drifts, the snow changed to slush, then mud and finally dirt. High snowbanks became porous ice and crusted by blown dirt seemed to shrink visibly with the lengthening days. As garden fences and ground emerged, the spit once again assumed its natural flatness. By the third week in April, darkness had gone from the night. Oswald came in with buckets of water gathered through widening cracks in the river ice. He took a duck from his jacket pocket.

"Here some 'spring' food for you."

"Thanks a lot. That'll taste mighty good," Fred noted a single shot in its neck. "Say, you are a real marksman!"

Oswald grinned. "Have to be. My son gonna be good hunter too. He kill his first game yesterday. Ptarmigan. We give it to him to eat tonight. Have friends in for kupiak (coffee). Want you come."

"Thanks, Oswald, we'd like to," Fred accepted. "Your boy isn't even in school yet, is he?"

Oswald shook his head. "Not yet. But shooting with rifle easier than old days. Used to hunt between bluff and Golovin. Eskimos get up early, find ptarmigan, chase 'em into air. Chase all day 'til ptarmigan too tired to fly. Have net up creek bed in alders and willows. Chase ptarmigan into net. Get a lot. Get a lot tired too."

As we talked, sounds of shouting came through the open window. A group of boys were playing a lively game much like soccer while around the edges of the square both sexes and all ages squatted over marbles.

"Sounds like a lot of fun out there," Fred observed.

"Yes, they have good time."

But spring for the Eskimos was also a time of serious activity.

In the days that followed, a migration took place. The hunters who had already returned to the village with seals, went out again for a final try. Some families took to the hills in search of greens and roots. Others went to gather bird's eggs on off-shore islands still connected to the mainland by a bridge of ice. And still others left for no other reason than that they had become restless with the winter's confinement. Daisy disappeared in the general exodus without giving notice. She simply failed to show up one day and we learned some time later that she had gone to snare squirrels.

Achebuk, back in the village with a year's supply of seal for his family, now came and offered to take us hunting. We agreed to leave the end of the week. Meanwhile, there were pictures to be taken of the reindeer herds which had come to the coast north of Unalakleet for spring fawning.

The regular overland trail leading directly to the area was now unfit for travel, with the snow all melted and the tundra spongy and abounding in bogs. Our alternative was to go along the beach where there was still hard-packed snow —a fine choice until we came to the first of a series of creeks emptying into the Bering Sea. Their spring flooding had melted the snow and cut deep chasms in the beach, forcing us to turn onto the sea ice where we found the roughest going of all. Here, a whole winter's accumulation of pressure ice had jammed close inshore and as we crashed sideways and down and skidded around, I thought the sled would fall apart. The shock was somewhat alleviated by gripping the sides of the sled and raising myself in a sort of posting motion but Fred had numerous bruises and some painfully stubbed toes before the trip was over. In between each obstacle course of pressure ice, the snow had blown and frozen into uneven ridges. We were tempted to go farther out where a new, smooth field had formed, but it was webbed with cracks and there was an offshore wind blowing. At times, the open water of the Bering Sea made a dark band between ice and sky. It was no more than a mile away.

Once in the locale of the reindeer, we decided to leave the sled and set out on foot over the tundra. We found the herds grazing among a few snow patches still remaining on the shady sides of hills.

The herder in charge was Richard Ioogiak, a young man strong and tanned by the sun. He was employed by the Government Native Service to protect the deer from prowling animals, chiefly wolves. Richard offered to help us in any way he could. In spite of this photographing the reindeer turned out to be a bigger problem than we had anticipated. Obligingly enough, they allowed us to creep close and focus our cameras, but at the first click of the shutter, the entire herd would turn as one and daintily trip away. With fine precision, they gauged their spurts to stop just out of camera range, necessitating our moving forward and setting up again. Yet they never went too far away to discourage us completely. We couldn't decide whether they were shy of us or possessed of a fiendish sense of humor. After almost three hours of fruitless stalking, we decided to resort to tactics.

While Fred and I concealed ourselves beneath bushes in a gully, Richard with the help of his dog, drove the herd around the hill toward our cameras. We had high hopes of some startling close-up action shots but the deer outsmarted us again. To be sure, they thundered around the hill as planned, but, instead of charging head on, they came from behind and before we could change about, had passed us by to stop—exactly out of range again. All we succeeded in filming were herds of deer-behinds bobbing in mockery. Added to our general discomfort were the swarms of mosquitoes which bedeviled us. We hadn't realized they had arrived with spring, because the wind kept us free of them in Unalakleet.

Then, we stumbled on to some extraordinary luck—a fawn being born. We were able to get his wide-eyed wonder at

the strange new world about him and the first creaky steps he took. Another fawn wobbled over to investigate but the mother deer became anxious and, prodding and nuzzling, guided her baby to the herd. It made a lovely little sequence. Now we packed our cameras and, turning our backs on the recalcitrant herd, took our departure bobbing in mockery. Wearily we boarded our sled and started the long, rough trip back. Out on the ice field, the late evening sun was turning myriad pools into a patchwork quilt of lavender and pink.

"There's an old-time Eskimo grave," Fred pointed out a pile of driftwood high on the beach. Stacked on end, it looked like a shock of corn silhouetted against the sky. "The body is placed on the top of the ground and the wood put over it. Ugh," he grunted as we hit another mound of pressure ice. "Unalakleet's the only area on the coast where graves are made like that. This one's out of the village because the man committed suicide. I saw—" but the sentence was never finished for at that moment Spotty and Slicker disappeared. They had gone into a three-feet-wide crack in the ice. Fred leaped from the runners and across the lead to hold Blackie, who had miraculously cleared the open water. I grabbed our cameras and deposited them some feet away, then I ran to give Fred a hand. Together, we pulled Blackie forward so that the towline helped Spotty and Slicker climb onto the ice. They were crying pitifully. We knew the dogs to be deathly afraid of the cruelly cold water, still there was nothing to do but pull Malibu and Homer through, too. Fortunately the sled runners were long enough to span the break and we came through without damage. It had happened so fast, there was no time to be frightened but once we were safe, I shook from head to foot. The sobering part about it was that it could happen again at any time. The lead had been completely concealed from us and the dogs by a rise in the ice field and a blind turn around pressure ice. It was just our good fortune the ice had not opened farther.

"Ready to go?" Fred asked at length.

I nodded. Once more I was able to draw a deep breath. "I suppose our dog sledding days are about over aren't they?"

Fred shook his head. "No. We'll still go on that seal hunt. With leads like this in the ice, seals will be coming up to sun themselves all over the place. You *do* want to go, don't you?"

"You bet I do." Already I was picturing a new pair of gloves made from the sealskin we would bring back. They would be the shape of a wolf's head, with the thumb for an ear, and would be the envy of all the girls in the village.

THE HUNT

Chapter V

THE SEAL HUNT

THE RUNNERS OF OUR HEAVILY LOADED SLED cut through two inches of newly fallen snow as we crossed the square and came to the beach. Achebuk was there, giving a last touch of seal oil to his snowshoes.

"Achebuk ready to go now. Snowshoes and sled all greased. Snow won't hurt."

"Will this snow spoil our chances of getting seal?" I asked.

"No. It good. A wet snow, late April, make warm blanket for baby seal." He lashed the sled upon which the borrowed kayak rested to the back of our sled and we were ready. Camping equipment and supplies for a week made a big load for the dogs but this was lightened somewhat as I trotted beside Fred.

Today, the North was at its best. The beach and ice field, freshened by the sprinkling of snow, lay luminous in the morning sun. At the horizon, cumulus clouds piled one on top of the other like tumbleweed against a fence.

Achebuk directed the dogs toward the edge of the ice field for here was our best chance of finding seal. Skirting the many pools of melted snow and ice, we came to the Bering Sea, a smooth, solid sheet of lapis lazuli. As we turned left

77

and continued along the water's edge, Achebuk must have sensed my apprehension. "It all right. Ice plenty strong. Maybe two, three feet thick."

With this comforting thought, I caught up to Fred instead of trailing behind.

"It landlocked too. No danger long as wind not blow anyway," Achebuk further reassured me.

We jogged along at a leisurely rate all morning—stopping to scan the water for seal at frequent intervals. None were to be seen. It was mid-afternoon when Achebuk suddenly clamped his foot on the claw brake between the runners and stopped the dogs without a spoken command. Motioning for us to be quiet, he pointed to a small seal lying some 100 yards ahead at the edge of the ice. Though the dogs quivered with the scent of it, they stayed in place while Achebuk pulled his rifle from the opening of the kayak and eased himself to the ground. Inch by inch he bellied to within ten yards of his quarry, all the while shielding his face with his fur mitt.

Slowly, slowly he brought his rifle up to fire. Simultaneously the seal took alarm, raised its head to sniff the air and slithered the few inches into the water.

Now Achebuk jumped up and came running, full speed, back to the sled. Without wasting words he unhitched the kayak sled and pulled it to the edge of the water. Quickly, he unlaced the skin boat from its carrier, launched it, lowered himself into the opening and paddled toward the spot where the seal had last come up for air.

Fred and I had never stalked game with anything more deadly than a camera but the sight of Achebuk paddling his kayak with infinite ease and grace, gliding and scanning the pure blue waters, gave us a deep vicarious thrill of the hunt. Easily and with great care, he racked his paddle on ivory hooks at the side of the craft and picked up his harpoon. There was a quick recoil and a forward thrust of the arm followed by a great thrashing in the water next to the kayak.

"Got 'im! Got 'im!" Achebuk yelled triumphantly.

He played the seal a few minutes, then turning, paddled to the edge of the ice dragging it behind him at the end of a length of thong. With the agility of a trained athlete, he scrambled out on the ice and pulled in the seal—a small one which lay quivering at his feet. Deliberately, Achebuk dropped beside it and crushed its skull with his fist. When he was certain the seal was dead, he could not refrain from showing delight. He jumped up rubbing his hands together.

"That good! That good! Fur of baby seal soft and white. Make good trim for parka. Maybe my woman make new parka!" The more he mulled over these thoughts the happier he became. In pure exaltation, he started dancing.

Spirits high we started out again but had gone only a few miles when we came to smooth new ice. Achebuk stopped the dogs. This would have to be tested before we ventured on it. Slipping into his snow shoes, he advanced cautiously, tapping the ice ahead with his ice pick before each step. He went some distance before returning to pronounce it safe for us, yet it was with little enthusiasm I stepped from the old ice onto the new.

"It all right," Achebuk insisted. "It about six inches thick. Long as east wind not blow, we safe."

Still I hesitated to go farther.

"Your woman afraid of ice?" he asked Fred.

"She's just not used to it."

"She get used to it. Eskimo heart beat differently out on ice too."

We had gone perhaps an eighth of a mile farther when Fred stopped us with an excited whisper.

"There's a seal, Ach."

Sure enough, far out in the water, a pointed nose came up for air, then disappeared. Instead of reaching for his rifle, Achebuk began scraping his ice pick on the ice. With this noise, he tried to lure the seal closer in to investigate since it was too far out to be pursued in a kayak. The ruse failed. The seal bobbed up again much farther out and that was the last we saw of him.

We decided to stop for awhile. Here the currents had corraled scores of ice floes and we hoped some seal might choose one of them for a sunbath.

"Have you ever had any trouble getting seals?" Fred asked.

"*Naga,*" Achebuk answered, never taking his eyes from

the sea. "I always get seal. I learn to hunt from my father when I no longer than harpoon. He learn from Eskimo up North. They learn from polar bear."

"From polar bear?"

"Eskimo learn to be quiet. To move quiet. To crawl. To shield face with mitt just like polar bear cover black nose with paw." Now Achebuk studied the floes through an old telescope which had been handed down in his family since the days of the Yankee whalers. "Sometimes get seal through seal hole."

"What's a seal hole?" I made myself comfortable against the kayak sled.

"It where seal eat his way through ice to breathe. Seal make hole this big," he indicated two inches. "Oogruk make bigger," this time his fingers would have gone around a grapefruit. "Stand over hole when tide go out, seal come up against tide. He turn like this," Achebuk rose, twisting his body in a spiral at the same time. "Harpoon him good," he brought his arm down in an imaginary thrust holding the pose just long enough to make sure we took note. Then he sat down and resumed his watch.

Finally, in late afternoon, he decided to go to the floes farther out and have a look around. While he paddled away Fred and I stretched out on the ice for a nap.

I awoke.

The air seemed colder. I took my arm from over my eyes and saw that a cloud was covering the sun. Fred was already sitting up and looking toward the northeast where the cumulus clouds had changed into ugly, black storm clouds. Just then a chilling breeze hit us.

"It's an offshore wind," he said anxiously.

In alarm, we looked out to sea. The water which had been like glass was heaving in long swells and breaking into whitecaps. There was no sign of Achebuk.

"This ice field could break loose any minute," Fred voiced the thought we both feared. "We better get ready to go."

Together we ran to the sled and packed the equipment. The wind began to blow harder. Water lapped and splashed menacingly at the edge of the ice.

"Achebuk's going to have a tough time handling his kayak in this water," Fred worried. He paced back and forth straining to catch a glimpse of our friend, "—and he can't swim—"

"He can't? Why in the world didn't he ever learn?"

"No Eskimos swim." His voice sounded impatient but then it was a foolish question. "The water's too cold for them to learn."

Thoroughly roused, we tried to decide what to do. Should

we wait for Achebuk or should we start with dogs toward shore? Achebuk could always get to safety in his kayak. But if the ice we were on started drifting to sea, we would be helpless unless Achebuk happened to see us in time and could transfer us atop his kayak. Still, that would be risky in the choppy water and our dogs, sleds and supplies would be lost. We told ourselves the sensible things was for us to start for shore at once—a decision we had no desire to follow until we knew Achebuk was safe.

Just then a black object nosed out from an ice cake—the bow of the kayak! Achebuk was coming in and he was fighting the waves with every stroke of his paddle. It took skill enough to handle a kayak in calm water but in the stormy Bering Sea an almost superhuman sense of balance was required. All about the light skin boat, ice floes bobbed like egg shells.

There were no glad halloos. Everyone was too tense. We stood on the ice field and held our breath as Achebuk guided the narrow craft at the exact angle to ride the swells. Finally, about twenty yards from us, he paddled in between our ice field and a large floe which afforded him some protection but threatened disaster should it suddenly move in.

We were both on hand to help Achebuk slip out and to lift the kayak out of the water.

"Are we glad to see you!" Fred exclaimed.

"Rough water," Achebuk said beginning to lash the kayak on its sled. "We hurry. East wind not good."

I jumped into the sled. With Achebuk on the runners and Fred running alongside, we raced full speed toward shore. At first glance the field looked serenely smooth and then we saw it—and our hearts stood still—far in the distance, a thin black line meandered from north to south and out of sight. The ice field had cracked! And the section we were on was drifting out to sea impelled by a steady offshore wind. We were stranded!

"Open water," Achebuk's grim tone underlined the dread we all felt.

"What'll we do, Ach?" I tried to keep my voice steady.

"We go see how wide it is," he told me between shouts to the dogs to go faster.

The closer we came to the lead, the wider it appeared. With growing dismay, we drew alongside to find 14 feet of open water separating us from safety.

Without losing a second, Achebuk turned the dogs left and started following the lead in hopes it had not widened as much farther on. Speed was imperative now, for though the ice field moved slowly in the beginning, it would gain momentum with each passing minute. If we could not find a place to cross, we stood to lose our dogs, our sleds and supplies. Except for repeated exhortations to the team from all of us, we sped along in silence, our eyes fixed on the yawning black water. Imperceptibly at first, then noticeably, the chasm began to narrow. We hardly dared think it might come together enough for us to cross but after long minutes of agonized hoping, we came to a place measuring not more than four feet. It was our only chance. Beyond that, the space widened again.

"Well, here goes," Fred took a sprint, jumped and was across. He held out an arm to me and running for all I was worth, I jumped toward him and to safety.

Together, we called the dogs to follow. For a moment it

looked as if they might but at the very edge of the ice, they balked and could not be coaxed to make the leap. Achebuk flailed at them and barked orders, but it was no use. In desperation, he grabbed the lead dog, Blackie, by the collar, dragged him to the rim and jumped. They made it! To our enormous relief we watched the rest of the team leap across followed by the sleds and kayak. Once we were all safe again on shorebound ice, my knees buckled. I sank to the ice in nervous exhaustion but as I went down I saw Fred grinding away at his camera!

He came over and pulled me up. There was no time to rest, for Achebuk had decided we should return to the village as quickly as possible. With an east wind blowing and the ice weakened by rough water, the entire field might go at any time.

We traveled far inshore, all of us walking to save the dogs and sinking into slush up to our ankles. Instead of taking time to skirt the pools of surface water, we sloshed directly through them. Bad as it was, this was a better trail than the beach almost completely barren of snow and littered with ice cast up by previous storms.

By early evening the wind had died down and the sun reappeared to cast long shadows on the golden snow. I saw Fred stop and study the tracks left by the dogs and when I came up beside him I saw them too—telltale spots of pink. Achebuk called the team to a halt while we all gave anxious inspection to their paws. We found, as we feared, their pads cut by sharp points of melting ice. We took out the boots brought along for just such an emergency and tied them securely on all the dogs. At first, they hesitated to touch their booted paws to the ground and danced around as if the snow were hot. Once we started out again, they didn't seem to notice any difference.

This time both Fred and Achebuk pushed the sled, for Homer's paws had been so badly cut we allowed him to run out of harness—a circumstance which completely transformed his personality.

A plodding, unimaginative, dun-colored work dog, he suddenly was transformed. His tail shot straight up in the air, his ears became erect triangles for the first and only time in his life. Loping just ahead of the hard working dogs and men, he gloried in his new found eminence with haughty leers and taunting barks. Perhaps in his own mind, Homer was leading the team in the epic serum run to Nome. At any rate, the show he put on was good for a laugh—our only one— on that wearisome trudge back to the village.

When we finally unhitched the team around ten that night, we knew it was for the last time. The ice was too dangerous for any trips from then on.

The same storm which cut short our seal hunt now brought the villagers hurrying home from their spring camping.

Soon sealskins, laced to frames like rugs in a loom, began to appear throughout the village. Thong cut in unbroken lengths up to fifty feet festooned the fish racks.

Miowak came by to tell us she was going to make a seal poke and hastily gathering up camera equipment, we accompanied her home. This was something we had long wanted to see, for it was an intricate operation involving a great deal of dexterity, since the entire inside of the seal was removed intact through its mouth.

She had prepared for the job by placing the dead seal on an oogruk skin spread in the deep green grass beside her house. Moreover, she had adorned herself with her most prized possession, a string of blue glass beads once used by the Russians in trading for furs.

When we were set, she dropped to her knees beside the animal and adroitly working her crescent bladed ooloo down its throat, cut between the muscles and the outer skin. Carefully she severed the tendons to the flippers, manipulating the knife with her right hand and kneading the skin over the blade from the outside with the left. While she worked, she kept up a running conversation with herself in native, punctuated with smiling, laughing or exclaiming as she reacted to her own comments.

Surprisingly enough, the procedure of making the poke did not seem gory, as there was very little blood. From time to time, Miowak fastidiously wiped the excess oil from her arms with handfuls of grass. Once she had made sure all the inner organs and muscles were cut loose, she turned the seal tail toward her. Then taking a front flipper in each hand and thrusting her foot forward against the hind end of the seal, she forced it inside out. Now the sealskin was an empty bag and the first phase of the job completed. Miowak stood up unconsciously striking a regal pose as she waited for us to gather our equipment. She had performed an onerous but necessary task yet she had lost not one whit of dignity in the doing of it.

After we left, the natural openings of the skin would be stitched closed and the bag inflated and allowed to dry. In time, it would be put to a variety of uses, the most common one being as a storage vessel for seal blubber while it rendered into oil. Sometimes, pokes were used as carryalls; often as floats in whale hunting. By tying an inflated poke to the other end of thong attached to a harpoon head, hunters were able to follow their whale once it was hit.

The villagers were just finishing the planting of their flower gardens the first week in May when the herring run started. While it was on, whole families worked the clock around, netting, cleaning and hanging the fish on racks to dry.

Daisy wandered into our kitchen one morning, hung up her coat, put on an apron and without a word started to work. That some sort of explanation was in order never occurred to her. Briefly, I considered teaching her a lesson in responsibility with a summary dismissal, but only briefly. It happened the dishwasher hired to replace her had just taken leave without notice and dishes were accumulating so—Daisy was re-employed forthwith.

This was no time for pointing a moral, anyway, for it was nearing break-up time and the break-up of the Unalakleet River was one of the two most important events we had planned to photograph. Since our movie was to be a documentary of life in the village from freeze-up in fall through the spring break-up, we simply had to get the outgoing river ice to end it. We knew to do so would require a constant vigil on the river, because there was no predicting at what exact moment the ice might choose to break. But that it would occur in May, we were certain.

With Daisy back holding down the kitchen, we started getting ready.

ESKIMO MOTHER

CHAPTER VI

BECOMING A SOURDOUGH

ALL ALASKA AWAITED BREAK-UP—the time when winter's
accumulation of ice would heave and grind down mountain
streams and out of headland lakes and, gathering momentum
like an avalanche, roll the length of larger rivers to the open
sea.

It would be the official beginning of spring.

In Unalakleet, the effects of break-up would be immediate
and far-reaching. Travel would be by boat instead of dog sled.
Fishing could be carried on without chopping through the ice
and the village would be clean again with water available for
washing and for carrying away the refuse piled behind each
cabin. Bush pilots would land in the river on floats instead of
on skis. Soon would come the ships with a year's supplies.
Break-up along with freeze-up had more effect upon Eskimo
living than any other occurrence in nature.

Break-up had a special significance for me, too.

With the break-up, I would become an Alaskan Sourdough
and that was an ambition grown out of my first meeting with
Fred. Introductions were scarcely over before he had revealed
that two levels of society existed in Alaska. There were the
newly arrived greenhorns or "Cheechakos" as they were

91

called, and there were the "Sourdoughs," the Alaskans who had what it took to stay. Since I had been in Alaska less than a week at the time, I was particularly sensitive of this distinction.

"How long would one have to stay in Alaska to become a Sourdough?" I had wanted to know.

"Well, there are two schools of thought on the subject," Fred had told me. "One holds to three requirements—to spit in the Yukon, to rub noses with a native and to kill a grizzly bear. But that's too easy," he went on. "Any tourist could fly up here and become a Sourdough in a week's time according to that. I go by the old timer's rule that you have to stay through an Alaskan winter, from freeze-up in fall through the spring break-up, before you're a real Sourdough."

Perhaps unknown to me, Fred was even then laying groundwork for my coming to Unalakleet. Perhaps not. But certainly, as he enlarged on the subject, explaining the word "Sourdough" had originated with the prospectors carrying a yeast starter in their packs for making bread, it came to embody all the hardy ruggedness and adventurous spirit of those early day pioneers. I was fired with an ambition to stay through an Alaskan winter and join the ranks of genuine Alaskan "Sourdoughs." And this was the reason I looked forward to break-up with eagerness quite aside from our imperative need photographically.

Although we'd made arrangements for our Eskimo friends to notify us at the first movement in the ice, by the eighth of May we could restrain ourselves no longer and started taking daily hikes up the banks of the Unalakleet River to look for ourselves. A sweet, fresh odor of moist earth filled the air and everywhere there was the sound of trickling water—in the tundra, on the beach, at the river's edge.

We knew the ice over feeder streams was already crumpling and pushing into the upper channels of the river and that this would start a chain reaction. Once the pressure from these expulsions became great enough, winter's shell over the headwaters would buckle and break adding to the pressure of the accumulating ice. Then this mass, building up with ice gouged from its path, would force its way irresistibly to the sea.

From our daily inspections, we concluded the river ice in the flats back of Unalakleet would offer little resistance to the oncoming mass. It was spongy and rotten, with pools of water covering the surface and cracks running in every direction. But down at the river mouth, there was still what appeared to be a solid section of ice forming a blockade from shore to shore. Here, the real joust between winter's ice and spring's outpouring would take place.

Consequently, when we received word on May 13th that the ice was beginning to move downriver, we took up our vigil on the banks overlooking this solid ice barrier at the river mouth. It was 6 p.m. and too dark for pictures. This was a gnawing worry, still if break-up was really coming, we didn't want to miss seeing it.

But nothing happened, then or the next day or the next.

As we watched hour after hour, the air became colder, the sky heavily overcast. By the third day, we were getting awfully tired of hard tack and tea and a little dazed from lack of sleep.

And then, finally that night we heard what sounded like a

steady drum roll in the distance coming closer and closer. We strained to see through the lingering twilight and made out a huge wall of jumbled ice stretching completely across the river and behind it, pent up muddy waters spilling over the river banks and flooding the marshland.

Gradually, the drum roll increased to a reverberating roar as the mass slowly advanced in gargantuan lurches, only to stop a bare quarter of a mile away. All was quiet again.

For some moments, we stared awed and unbelieving.

"It's getting powerful close," Fred said. "Don't know if that ice at the river mouth will hold till daylight or not."

That night we didn't bother to undress, since we were both too keyed up to sleep. By 2:30 a.m. we were up and out again. To our relief, the wall was exactly where it had been when we left only now there was a deep, constant rumble emanating from it.

Fred studied his meter and discovered there was enough light for taking movies, even though the sky was gray. "You can put the show on any time now," he told the complaining mass upriver. Still the wall took its own time.

Not until four hours later did it begin to come to life in giant spasmodic tremors. After each tremor, the mass would settle amid amplified rustlings and scraping of ice but with each settling there would be a relentless, insidious encroachment upon the ice at its base. Thus, the wall unremittingly built up its forces for a final thrust to the sea. And watching all this from the river bank, our excitement built up as surely as the pressure of that laboring mass.

The Eskimos were as fascinated by the struggle of the ice as we, even though it was an annual event for them. From the

time we'd taken up our vigil, they had come by twos and threes to watch. There were some half dozen standing around that morning when suddenly whole upper sections of the wall began to totter and break off and crash ahead.

At the same moment, the entire mass of ice started forward, crunching and grinding inexorably downriver. With the power of a battering ram, it hurtled into the blocking ice at the river mouth. There was a series of thunderclaps and earth-shaking shudders as the river ice buckled and broke, accompanied by sounds like rifle shots and the roar of swollen water. Mortally shaken by the first blow, the remaining ice gave way. Quietly as a shrug and with magnificent sweep, it floated majestically out to sea, propelled from behind by a cauldron of churning trees, rocks and ice.

With the first buckling of the ice, several children had run to spread the word. "Break-up! Break-up!"

Now all the villagers rushed down to the river to witness the phenomenon which was to change their way of life until the waters froze again in fall. Fred came over and gave me a hug.

"You're a Sourdough now. Congratulations!"

Until late afternoon, we presided, along with the villagers, over the disgorgement. We had fought this battle of break-up step by step from the first tentative nudge many miles back in the hills. As the ice mass increased and moved, so had our pulses quickened to the advance. When the spectacular clash at the river mouth took place, we had been a part of it and with the final egress of the ice, we had known the elation of victory. Now we felt only relief that it was over—and a pervading weariness. Still we watched as trees and rocks whirled past less and less often, and finally not at all. And when the late evening sun was turning the tundra to rust-gold, we saw a solitary cake of ice proceed in stately fashion to the sea. It was a sign to us—a sign that spring had officially come.

Now we gave our attention to packing furs, clothes, camera equipment and paintings into five large sea-chests. We had heard that a ship, the *Reefknot*, had left Seattle on May 3rd for Nome, with a scheduled stop in Unalakleet on the return trip. Once the Trading Post supplies were lightered ashore and our freight put aboard, all that remained for us to do was turn the key back to Uncle Charlie, who was due to arrive the latter part of May. But Uncle Charlie had long since tired of the noise and hurry of the States.

"*Kokturok*," as he was called by the Eskimos, stepped off the plane May 19th. Hellos had hardly been said before he was urging us to stay until the *Reefknot* came. It didn't take us long to make up our minds. Fred knew he could be of help in lightering and I was glad to have the chance to get to know Uncle Charlie better for he was one of the pioneers who had helped to build Alaska.

Uncle Charlie had first come North from California to trade but not a year of his half century's stay had passed that he hadn't grubstaked one or more prospectors—without success. He had the distinction of being the oldest operating trader on the west coast of Alaska and though his life had been a solitary one, it had been significant to those about him. Always sought for advice, often for credit and favors, he also gave freely of himself when needed. In 1919, he had nursed the village through a siege of influenza almost singlehandedly. He had lived rigorously, yet for all his eighty-two years, he was an active, alert individual whose favorite pastimes were listening to news over the battery radio and playing cribbage.

Now that Uncle Charlie was in charge of the trading post again, we started hiking up to CAA in the evenings to develop our film at Norm and Romayne Potosky's apartment. Norm and Romayne were a husband-wife communicator team who had come to Alaska during World War II.

Realizing the limitations of our gasoline lamps and mixing bowls in developing film, they were kind enough to offer us the use of their running water, electricity and a dark room improvised from their kitchen. At the same time, they placed their shower at our disposal, a situation we accepted with alacrity.

Freshly showered and bearing a large batch of newly developed negatives, we were returning from the Potosky's one evening when we met a woman pushing a wheelbarrow. As she pulled to a stop in the deep grass beside the path, we could see her load was a single huge salmon.

"Salmon starting to run," she informed us.

This proved to be the case not only in the Unalakleet River but in waters all over Alaska. That same week, Gren Collins, veteran bush pilot, came to enroll the villagers for work in salmon canneries. My Malemute teacher, Dave Panipchuk who was one of those to go, came to tell us good-bye.

"What would you like me to send you from the States?" I asked.

"A dictionary," he replied without hesitation. I had one with me and gave it to him and the profuse gratitude with which he thanked me made me feel guilty over the smallness of the gift.

Monday dawned clear and warm—good flying weather. The plane would stop today.

We ate a late breakfast with Uncle Charlie and visited with our Eskimo friends who dropped in to say good-bye. Achebuk promised when we came back, he would kill enough oogruk to make a kayak for each of us. Miowak, Fred's foster mother, brought us a treasured wooden spoon. Daisy, my wayward dishwasher, gave out large and unsubtle hints to be taken along. Oswald, Lowell, Kootuk, Frank and the Ivanoffs all crowded in to wish us good luck while Kyrok, who could not speak English, pressed our hands against her cheek and smiled her good-byes.

It should have been gay but we found our lips stiff with the smiles we didn't feel. We went out and gave our dogs a final petting and then our group, which had grown into a noisy delegation, started the walk to the airstrip. Vegetable gardens were now flourishing, the tundra surrounding the airfield had become a palette of wild flowers.

We waited only a few minutes before the plane swooped down and glided to a halt.

"Good-bye, good-bye! *Berahin* (good-bye to you). *Berahitchee* (good-bye to everyone)."

We found our seats in the plane and sat with our faces pressed against the window. Even across the field, we were sure we could catch the twinkle in Uncle Charlie's blue eyes. Tall, erect, he stood out from everyone else and as long as we could see anyone at all, he was waving us on to good luck "outside."

I turned to Fred with eyes brimming. He was taking pictures!

Finally he put down the camera and I could see that he was deeply touched, too.

We both took one more look out of the window. In that eternally compelling land of blue ice, flowering tundra and Eskimos, we had left a part of our hearts.

OLD SOURDOUGH

Chapter VII

OUR FIRST LECTURES

We were back in civilization.

And all the things we had once taken for granted, we saw again with sharpened perception, as for the first time.

I remember the luxurious softness of the taxicab cushions in Anchorage and the miracle of an elevator going up with the press of a button.

I remember the noises—of fire engines and screeching brakes and diesel whistles and smells—of chlorinated water and drug store cosmetic counters; and fresh milk and vegetable salads and day-old eggs which tasted a litle flat after our aged ones at Unalakleet.

I remember the thrill of sailing through Southeastern's countless fiords and standing at the ship's rail watching the disappearing Alaskan shoreline and Fred saying, "We'll come back. We'll come back and make our home some day."

And the trip across Canada in a single berth in order to save money. And the heat of Minneapolis and Chicago because all the clothing we had were woolens and thick Alaskan blood pounded in our temples.

And then Fred's mother saying, "Welcome to Ohio."

And seeing my husband for the first time in a hat and a

starched shirt. And walking on high heels again and feeling tall and tottery.

And then the lecture season was upon us.

Our first lecture was in California, with no dates on the way out or back, but that year we took anything our manager offered.

It was just as well we had no appearances on the way, for the show wasn't ready. We simply hadn't allowed ourselves enough time to edit the film or work out any sort of lecture to go with it. We made the trip with me holding the typewriter on my lap, taking down a lecture Fred dictated as he drove. At night, we would set up our projector in our room and coordinate the speech we'd composed during the day with the movie, which was cut as we went along.

Three hours before showtime, we arrived on the coast, completely unstrung but with what we hoped would pass as an illustrated lecture. We changed into our evening clothes and went out for dinner only to encounter a difficulty entirely foreign to either of us—the food wouldn't go down. In a spirit of walking our last mile, we proceeded to the theater, Fred muttering parts of his speech interspersed with strong expressions of regret that he'd ever thought of lecturing.

When we arrived we found the theater dark. After making certain we were at the correct address, we suffered agonies thinking this was the wrong night or that no one would show up.

But they came at last. First the projectionist, then the program chairman *and* to our complete amazement—an audience —enough to fill the auditorium.

Time ran out.

Pale, with palms slick, Fred stepped out to acknowledge his introduction ". . . great pleasure to present Mr. Matcheetang." It was the first of many variations on the pronunciation of Machetanz.

I watched from the projection booth so queasy I could scarcely hold my head up.

The lights dimmed, the movie started. In spite of the speech being ragged and the timing off, the pictures carried themselves for they were good pictures and our subject matter couldn't miss. Gradually I began to realize the audience was interested! Even more, it *liked* our show! Its first response was a reprieve to breathe again. Now I could listen to what Fred was saying and take notes for future lectures.

And then, without warning, the movie stopped, the theater went black and the nightmare was upon us again. After a startled pause, Fred began extemporizing on what had last appeared on the screen. Up in the projection booth everything was pandemonium. A main fuse had blown and no one knew where a replacement was.

"What will we do?" I moaned.

"I'll go downtown and see if any of the stores are still open and get one," and with that the projectionist was gone, falling down four concrete steps in his hurry.

For twenty interminable minutes, the theater was without lights and Fred talked, not knowing when the movie would start again or what was wrong. If anyone had offered us our expenses home, we would have given up lecturing on the spot and forever. But no one did.

Instead, the movie began running again and the show went on. When it was over, the program chairman came on the stage and thanked "Mr. Matcheetang" for his splendid show-manship in carrying on while the lights were out. There was an appreciative burst of applause from the audience. It was the sweetest sound we'd ever heard. We were goners.

And now came the best part of the show—when it was "buttoned up" and we could go out for a midnight snack and talk everything over with the good feeling of knowing our efforts had produced a measure of pleasure. Still it was three years and many lectures later before that good "after" feel-ing began to balance that bad "before" feeling.

There were many teeth to be cut along the way.

There was learning to arrive ahead in time to check the projection, for it might just be a machine for slides instead of movies, or the screen too small, or the film wound wrong or the operator nearsighted and unable to see the screen to focus.

There was learning that people like to laugh, that intro-ductions were important, that audiences who paid were more appreciative as a rule than those who didn't.

And there was heating water on the traveling iron to make coffee for breakfasts and luncheons packed in order to make ends meet. And driving all night to get back to Ohio because we had ordered steak instead of hamburger and the differ-ence meant a room.

There was the end of the first year and realizing with a hollow feeling we had lost instead of made money on our lecturing. The dream of returning to Alaska to build our home seemed far away indeed.

The wedding suit was made over, the Homburg reblocked and we were into our second season.

And that year there were milestones.

We saw a fellow lecturer's show—our first since we entered the business. We found to our immense surprise, that our audiences laughed just as much, clapped just as loudly and that our film compared favorably from a technical standpoint. It gave us a wonderful confidence. Now, we knew we would get there. It might take time to become established but we knew we had the show to make it.

We gave up our manager and hired a secretary to handle our booking and in so doing we set ourselves up in business—in a peculiar backhanded way.

It all came about because we needed a letterhead and when we asked ourselves what our business was, the answer was obvious—what we ourselves produced. We would be "Machetanz Productions" and since our output of painting, books, lectures, movies and photographs was all Alaskana, our slogan "The Graphic North" was ready made. Finally, we needed a trademark and here we made a play on our name, the pronunciation of which had given the lecture chairmen so much trouble. Of German origin, the name Machetanz translated into English meant "make a dance." To symbolize our business, Alaska, we chose an Eskimo and to symbolize our name, Fred sketched him "making a dance." From then on, our little dancing Eskimo appeared on all our letterheads, lecture brochures, movies and business cards and whether it was due to the trademark or not, our luck took a turn for the better.

The Alaskan Government commissioned Fred to do a documentary film of the Territory.

Now, at last, we could return to our hearts' home. Moreover, in making the movie we would point our cameras into every cranny of the Territory, an excellent opportunity for scouting that future homesite. And finally, we would do another thing we had long wanted—we would drive the Alaska Highway.

We started North in April. Spring! The earth throbbed with new life and our hearts kept time to its beat.

Left behind were the spring floods of the midwest, past farmers ploughing dark brown earth between strips of tan stubble, into the land of cowboy boots and silver dollars and sheep on far hills looking like plump larvae on the green blanket of spring.

Then to the Canadian border to be admitted in eight minutes and then through miles of wheat country and towering grain elevators standing like sentinels on the prairies; and beginning five quarts of gasoline to the gallon and imported woolens and restaurant shelves lined with teapots.

And seeing the aurora for the first time in two years stretching like welcoming arms across the northern sky.

At Dawson Creek, British Columbia, "0" mile of the Alaska Highway, we found a typical, bustling frontier town where the old and new met face to face. Soda fountains were equipped with all the chrome the railway which terminated there could bring in. There was a theater and modern restaurants with venetian blinds, yet teams of horses were a frequent sight on the main streets and water was sold in the outskirts for five cents a bucket with a special of sixty-five cents on a barrel.

We rented a hotel room and spent a grateful hour bathing, for after 400 miles of unpaved road, we were on intimate terms with dust. Our eyes burned with it, our nostrils were black holes, our hair looked like moles drying in the sun, every crease of our skin was a dust-filled line. There was even grit between our teeth. Still in the morning we retraced several dusty blocks to start our trip over the Alaska Highway from the "0" milepost—exactly 1523 miles from Fairbanks where it terminated.

The Alaska Highway began wide, well-graded and graveled with deep drainage ditches on either side. Our initial impression and one that proved correct was that the hazards of the trip had been highly exaggerated. There were stretches where the surface was washboardy and there were seasonal frost boils and some pot holes but nothing that remotely approached danger if one exercised judgment in speed. Depending upon immediate conditions we drove up to fifty miles an hour, yet others could and did go faster. The worst feature by far was the ever present dust but one could overlook this with magnificent scenery at every turn. Broad river valleys and countless lakes, still frozen, broke the vast forests of spruce, birch and aspen. Snow-covered ranges loomed in the distance while near, newer mountains told the story of earth's making in their sheer rock surfaces.

We did not see the wildlife we had expected, spotting only one cow moose and a lone eagle. What did appeal to us as much as the scenery were the personalities we met along the way. Each manager of every roadhouse—and roadhouses averaged less than fifty miles apart—had a story to tell.

At Lakeview Lodge overlooking Muncho Lake—beautiful though sealed with pistachio green ice—we met C. C. Brandt who had trapped for 31 years and established a world's record of 237 beavers in one season. Besides being a born naturalist, he was possessed of an innate "story sense" when relating experiences on his 150-mile trap line. We sat before a crackling open fire, listening.

He showed us how to call rabbits with a peculiar little sound and the thump of the foot. He told of killing moose while they slept, with a spear fashioned from the straightened spring of a #4 trap. Then he recounted a trip 175 miles into the Sikanni River some twenty years ago and the hardships he and his partner had encountered.

These were the men who had opened this country, trappers like Mr. Brandt, the traders to whom they took their furs and more lately lodge keepers along the Highway.

The Porsilds were a family who had established a lodge on the banks overlooking the Teslin River. While Mrs. Porsild turned out delicious Danish food for their dining room, her husband, a blond giant of a man, entertained wayfarers with tales of his travels by dog sled over northern Alaska and

Canada. At Christmas when the children were home from boarding school in Whitehorse they would take their one holiday of the year. A sign "Not Open For Business" would go up on the door and there would be a real Old Country celebration with much singing and a Christmas tree glowing in the light of real candles from Denmark.

Music, homemade with fiddle, guitar, accordion or harmonica was to be expected at any of the lodges once supper was out of the way. With radio reception poor or non-existent and no other source of entertainment available, these impromptu concerts filled a hungering need of the settlers. Whether the tune happened to be gay or sad, it was played and listened to with all the seriousness accorded the deepest stirrings of the soul.

The majority of lodges were built from remodeled Canadian Army barracks and one standard feature of their construction were openings at the ceiling and floor of each room to allow the circulation of heat from a main stove. As a result, there was no soundproofing and any illusions of privacy in bedroom or bath were shattered completely.

When we came to Milepost 917, the city of Whitehorse, we were on familiar ground. It was here, nearly three years before, Fred Machetanz on his way to spend a winter with his Uncle on the west coast of Alaska, had shown the sights to a tourist he had met the day before. From Whitehorse, the artist-photographer and the vacationer had happened to be on the same wood-burning stern-wheeler down the Yukon to historic Dawson. The spell of the Yukon had taken hold and by the end of the cruise, they had become engaged. Five months later they were married in the Eskimo village of Unalakleet.

In an overflow of sentiment, we retraced our hike out to Whitehorse Rapids on the Yukon River. Once again, we sat on the banks watching the swirling waters which the Indians had named "Whitehorse Rapids" because the white foam reminded them of the tails of white horses waving in the wind. Then, on to Miles Canyon where the river was spectacularly compressed between vertical walls of rock columns. On the way back to Whitehorse, we began to realize we'd walked a good many miles. We cut across to the Highway and thumbed a ride. That evening, we'd planned to go to the small servicemen's club where we had danced until 1:30 in the morning three years ago—the morning I had exclaimed:

"Oh, look at the moon!"

"That's not the moon!" Fred had laughed. "That's the sun coming up. Remember, you're in the land of the Midnight Sun now."

Since that time, we had both seen the Midnight Sun many times and besides that our feet were tired.

"Let's call it a day," Fred suggested after dinner and I readily agreed.

The fact that we had to be up by three a.m. had something to do with it, too. We were storing our car at Whitehorse for the time being to take the little narrow-gauge railroad across the mountains into Alaska.

And the reason the time for departure had been advanced by four hours was that this was the snow slide season and slides were less likely to occur in the early morning than in the afternoon following hours of softening by sunshine. But, of course, there was never any predicting when a snow slide would happen.

INDIAN HUNTER

Chapter VIII

BACK TO ALASKA

When the train pulled out at four o'clock the next morning, we were its only passengers.

The trip was one to stir the imagination, for the railroad followed the same route prospectors had taken from Skagway over the mountains through White Pass in the gold rush of 1898. The prospectors themselves had laid the track, riding from Skagway to the end of the line to work for a time as crewmen before pushing on by foot for the Klondike. From Whitehorse, the grade was a gradual ascent to Lake Bennett, where once a tent city of thousands had flourished. Now all that remained was the picturesque ruin of a chapel. It was here many of the gold seekers had taken to boats and crudely fashioned rafts to continue their trip by water to the Yukon.

Past the lake, we came into snow banked so high on either side of the tracks it was like going through a tunnel with the top lifted off. There was a brief stop at the Canadian-Alaskan border. Then we were in Alaska once more and the really spectacular part of the trip began.

Now barren yet softly contoured mountains pressed one behind the other, range upon range. A little farther on where these ranges failed to knit, a tenuous pass descended to the

sea. It was through this opening our little engine crawled, lizard-like, around and over sheer rock surfaces. At times, it seemed the mere rocking of the coach would send us crashing down the mountainside, so steep it simply dropped from sight. Added to this disquieting sensation was the real possibility of a snow slide. In passing each deeply carved draw, a roar of wind and rush of water would hit the car broadside. It was the exact sound of descending snow and I found myself bracing against the impending avalanche.

Conductor Harold E. Mulvihill finished his paper work and with brakeman, Jack Lee, took the seat opposite us. Mr. Mulvihill or Mickey as he asked us to call him, had a fresh scar across his face which he told us was from injuries sustained when pinned in the coach car in a snow slide just four months before. It was of that he talked while we gave searching glances up the snow-filled draws.

"It happened in January, on the 4th to be exact—I'll never forget it. It was about eleven in the morning when she let go. What a noise! It made your blood run cold! It turned the engine over. Burned the engineer bad from the steam. Jack here was in the observation tower and that broke all the way off and was buried in the snow down the mountain. He wasn't dug out for two hours, were you, Jack?"

The brakeman shook his head. "I never knew what happened—when it hit or when they took me out."

"Well, I guess it's better that way. Now take the slide in '47. There was a man killed in that one. I was in the Jordan spreader when she hit. I kept thinking of my boy in Skagway before they got me out and that time I prayed. Oh I'd prayed before all right, only this time I meant it."

As we zigzagged down the mountains, Mickey called our attention to passing points of interest. There was a tumbled down log cabin where a pioneer woman had made herself famous by cooking pies and selling them to the toiling packers. And a memorial to the faithful packhorses whose carcasses had once littered the trail.

"They say the smell was terrible," he added by way of further description.

Another, far different and more pleasant odor filled the air as we stepped off the train in Skagway. The Balm of Gilead trees were in full bloom, giving off a heady and exotic aroma in the sticky pods they shed. It was a sensation we were forever to associate with Skagway in spring.

From the station we went straightway to Pullen House.

This too had a sentimental attachment for it was here we had met. When I had first arrived in Skagway and gone to Pullen House, Fred had chanced to be at the door and showed me to the big desk built in a corner of the parlor.

The double doors of this old house, once a boarding place for prospectors, led into another century. There were the same overstuffed black leather teeter chairs which had squeaked accompaniment to tales of the trail. Brass spittoons that had caught the expertly aimed amber of hardy prospectors looked as expectant as ever. An octagonal table, buffed by countless moosehide pokes being pushed across its surface stood ready for business.

Now we found Pullen House closed. Ma Pullen had passed on and the hotel was run by her daughter in a new, more modern building. Before going there, we allowed ourselves a peep into the wing of the old house which had lately served as a museum. Three years before Ma herself had shown us through her treasure trove of old trunks, furniture and be-whiskered faces staring down from ornate frames. Though her hair had been completely white, she was even then much too alert to be considered a shade of the past. She had pointed to a cabinet resembling a modern day juke box.

"Do you know what that is?"

We couldn't guess. To our surprise, we'd learned it really was a juke box of ancient vintage with its needles scratching over metal cylinders and powered by a hand crank. Ma had turned to us. Eyes twinkling, she began to sing a gay unfamiliar song and then lifting her skirts just a trifle, she danced a little jig. We had watched in amazement as her high laced shoes tapped and circled. She had been an old, old lady cavorting among dust-covered relics but what we had seen was a younger, slimmer Ma Pullen dancing in a circle of home-sick, hungry-eyed adventurers.

Just as suddenly she had stopped. Her skirts dropped and the life went from her. She shook her head. "Good times," she had said over and over to herself as she left us.

But even though Ma Pullen was gone and her boarding house was no longer open for business, Skagway still retained a strong turn-of-the-century flavor.

As we walked down the main street, a man stepped out of a doorway just ahead of us. From peg top trousers to bat wing collar and four-in-hand, he was a dashing dude of the 90's. A ten-gallon hat shaded his face, the lower half of which was adorned with a heavy black mustache and well-trained goatee. Most splendid of all was a red satin vest spanned by a watch chain of gold nuggets as big as guinea eggs. We walked over and introduced ourselves and learned that the gentleman was Jack Kirmse, manager of a gift shop and that the mustache and goatee had been grown for a reason.

"It's a local custom," he grinned. "Everybody in Skagway dresses up in gay 90's clothes when the tourists come to town. There's a boat due this afternoon."

"Are those nuggets real gold?" I couldn't resist asking.

"They certainly are. This is the largest gold nugget watch chain in the world. It used to be owned by a gambler, Pat Renwick was his name. When he had a run of luck he wore this chain but when his luck turned bad, he borrowed on it from my father. I guess he ended up with his luck bad. The biggest one's worth $500."

Leaving Mr. Kirmse, we proceeded down the boardwalk

of Skagway's main street, across the railroad tracks and out to the docks. Here on a sheer rock bluff facing the waterfront were painted ship's insignia and flags of vessels from ports all over the world. As more accessible areas of the bluff had been used up, painting of insignia had become a standing challenge with each recently arived ship's crew trying to outdo all previous efforts. Ingenious sailors had rigged bosun's chairs from the cliff's top to paint their emblem the largest and most conspicuous of all—until the next ship put into port. Yet the effort which stood out from all the rest as we sailed from the harbor several days later was of local significance—a boldly painted skull of Soapy Smith, gambler, murderer and swindler of prospectors of '98.

We were passengers on a yacht. The vessel had originally been designed to accommodate some dozen persons including crew but in this instance it carried 57 church conference-bound youngsters and their chaperones. Since it was a mixed crowd with ages ranging from ten to twelve, there was much giggling and a great showing of affection with pinching, slapping and arm twisting. Sleeping arrangements were three to an upper bunk, four to a lower and once these were taken up the overflow distributed themselves on top of the table, three to the benches around the walls, one to the eight-inch-wide brace between the table legs and four to the floor. We were in the last named category and directly over the engines. We spent the night sitting up to cool our backs, which were virtually fried by daybreak.

In Ketchikan the weather was clear and when this occurred in Alaska's panhandle which averaged as much as 150 inches of rain a year, it was well to take advantage of it. We left

immediately on a Forest Service boat to photograph logging.

With us was forester Art Hodgeman whose appearance was that of an executive rather than an outdoor man except for his green Forest Service outfit. On the other hand, Captain Aiken who piloted the Forest Service boat looked the part of a sea-faring man exactly with a barrel chest and the inevitable cap pulled low to shade his eyes from the water's glare.

Southeastern was incomparably beautiful with hemlock, spruce and cedar-covered mountains rising at random out of the water and sunshine bouncing off every ripple of her innumerable fiords. We turned into a bay off one of these fiords and saw before us a small floating city. There was a bunkhouse and a mess hall and a workshop all on log rafts. Beyond them, another raft bearing machinery rested on a spit and between the spit and the shore, huge logs lay strewn on the beach prior to rafting.

Captain Aiken pulled to and made fast to the owner's boat anchored a little apart in the deeper water. It was three o'clock in the afternoon, the skies were clear and so began our photographing of Alaska's businesses, industries and recreation.

One of the first things we noticed was that no matter what the job, each man had a single characteristic of dress—the cuffs of his trousers had been ripped off and the ends frayed to barely reach the top of ankle high boots.

"Why?" I asked Art.

"So when he has to get out of the way of falling timber, his pants' cuffs don't catch on the underbrush. When they're frayed at the edges, they just tear farther. It's called 'stagging' the pants and they all do it before they put them on and go into the woods," he explained.

Art pointed out other dangers. He told us there was the possibility of the cable breaking with force enough to cut a man in half and at the same time warned us to stay clear of the "bight of the line," the cable vibration which could sever a leg and never pause in its arc.

"It's the toughest work there is," he continued, "but they make good pay and they do have all the comforts of home in their off hours—electricity, running water and always the best of food. The isolation's rough—still that's the best feature of all," he added. "Absolutely no place to spend their money."

There was another, more compulsive attraction Fred and I decided—the fundamental satisfaction that comes to strong men in fully realizing their physical strength.

Evenings, the four of us would gather in the galley. While Fred loaded cameras and labeled film and Art filled in his reports and I wrote up my notes, Captain Aiken would fix a "mug up" of coffee and placing it before us would start the talk.

"Well," he'd say. "What'd you learn about the side hill gougers today?"

"What are 'side hill gougers?' " I would ask knowing very well that was exactly what he wanted me to do.

"You mean you don't know that by now?" he acted surprised. "You've been seeing them every day. Next time you're out in the woods, you look sharp, you'll see the loggers all have one leg longer'n the other from gougin' the sides of mountains. Fact is if they ever came down to level ground, they'd probably only be able to go in a circle."

Then I'd see his eyes twinkling over the rim of his coffee mug and realize he was enjoying himself fully as much as we enjoyed listening.

"See any limb luggers?" he'd go on.

I shook my head. "What are limb luggers?"

"Why, they're the little gremlins that scatter limbs in the woods. I remember once at a show in Fitzgibbon Cove—" and he would be off on a tale, spiced with many succinctly phrased opinions and observations.

One morning we went to see a "roll up." Here in a well-protected cove, the logs rafted from nearby logging operations were built into huge rafts for towing to Alaskan lumber mills or as far away as Seattle.

Captain Aiken and I stood at the rail watching the loggers as they leaped among the floating logs, selecting which one was to be rolled up and once it was cabled, guiding it to its place on the raft. Each carried a long-handled spear hook used in breaking up jams and as an aid to balancing. A further aid were their spiked shoes called "corks" but these had little effect when the bark, rotted from long exposure to water, simply fell away at the slightest touch.

"Whups!" Captain Aiken jerked his head up as a figure teetered uncertainly, then in a frantic treading motion tried unsuccessfully to stay atop a rolling log. With a resounding splash he was in the water to scramble out just as quickly and continue working in dripping clothes. When the Captain saw he was safe, he finished his sentence, ". . . he sure punched a hole in the bay!"

"That looks like pretty dangerous work."

"It is. They have to build those rafts just right and even when they're on the way, they might rub together from the swell of the water and catch fire, but that doesn't happen often. Most of 'em get to the mill."

Photographing one of the mills to which these rafts were towed was our first project upon returning two days later. To our surprise, we found it provided colorful subject matter with bright yellow stacks of lumber set off by a background of rich green mountains.

These mountains not only formed a backdrop for the majority of cities in the Panhandle but determined a similar characteristic construction. Since they rose abruptly from the water's edge, there was no direction for cities to expand but up. As a result, houses clung to slopes so steep that from above, their roofs looked like awnings attached directly to the mountainside. Instead of sidewalks, wooden steps led down to the main part of town, squeezed between the mountains and the water front, and here was the most decorative touch of all—the fishing fleets at anchor in their harbor.

In such photogenic setting we hunted out the small businesses of Southeastern—fur farming, candy making, the custom designing of furniture and the arts and crafts of the Southeastern Indians. There was old Casper Mather chiseling totems with an ancient adze and talking of the Great Spirit turning cowards into humped-back salmon and there was young George Mather carving miniature totems in a workshop equipped with the latest in electrically powered machinery and telling us of his regular job at the lumber mill. The Indian women excelled in sewing moccasins, trimmed with intricate beadwork of their own design and putting together waxed crepe paper corsages which looked as real as the flowers growing lush and large in Southeastern flower gardens. A more modern craft was the building of fine fishing boats by Rod Davis, Mayor of Metlakatla, a small village on the island Indian reservation bearing the same name. The boat he was working on, Mayor Davis informed us in impeccable English, would go to a sportsman in Idaho, but not all of his orders went so far. There were many Davis Craft plying Southeastern waters under the guiding hand of local fishermen.

It was a fish-happy area where boats were as common as cars, where "Gone Fishing" signs appeared with recurring frequency on the doors of professional offices and where each year fishing Derbys were held with prizes running into thousands of dollars.

We went fishing ourselves—not for the salmon but for trout.

Lee Ellis and his wife, Alice, who guided fishing parties between big game hunts took us in their outboard motor boat some twenty miles up the Stikine River. The scenery looked as if it had been lifted from a book of fairy tales with a slight mist softening the edges of castle-shaped mountains and tinting them pastel hues. At every bend there was a different, yet equally tranquil vista to set us exclaiming but we weren't the only rubberneckers on the river that day. Now and then a hair seal would pop his head out of the gray, glacial water, look all around and submerge again. Lee pointed to one with his pipe.

"They sure can wreck a fish net or a trap for that matter."

"Aren't they used for anything around here?" I asked, thinking how indispensable these same animals were to the Eskimos.

"Nope. All they're good for is the six dollar bounty."

Later we stopped and ate our fill at a strawberry patch a homesteader had planted long ago and left, and then we were on our way again to turn off shortly into a quiet, brown slough between an almost perfect hedge of alders. Another turn and we were in the Ellis' fishing stream where the water ran white and was dappled with sunshine and the banks were etched with tracks of bear, moose, beaver and mink.

Just when we were beginning to think we had seen every variety of scenery Southeastern had to offer, Lee took us to the headwaters of his stream, where we found the loveliest, most perfectly composed picture of all. There in the center of a meadow of tall waving grasses was a lake reflecting in minute detail distant snowy crags rising above a forest of spruce. "Paradise Lake" it was called and we tucked the memory of it in our mental file of possible homesites.

We returned to Lee's cabin by the stream where trout were so plentiful, they could be seen darting from under the banks and rocks. With a strike at every cast Lee and Alice made, there was soon a good mess for supper accompanied by corn-bread, onions, strong hot coffee and the relaxed talk that goes with a fishing trip. The conversation turned to bear—a subject Lee could speak on with authority for though no older than mid-thirties in appearance, he had had many experiences with "brownies" in his years of trapping, hunting and guiding.

"Yeah, I had a bear attack me once," he responded in answer to our question. "Happened last spring and he took a souvenir," he rubbed his thigh meaningfully. "The bears had just come out of hibernation. Their coat's better then—more sleek and not so worn. I had a fellow out hunting and he wounded a good sized brownie but it got away before either of us could finish it off. Well, you don't want an outlaw around so we had to trail it," Lee paused. It was easy to vis-ualize him studying the signs and scents and sounds, moving into the brush, lithe as the animal he stalked. "I was walking several paces in the lead when we came to a rise. Just as I started up, my hunter yelled 'There's a bear!' I thought he meant it was coming up behind so I turned and just as I did, the wounded bear came charging over the rise. He hit me so hard, it knocked my rifle right out of my hands. We both— the bear and me—rolled over and over and when we ended up he was on top with one foot on my chest and one here," he indicated his shin, "and my thigh was between his teeth."

"What did you think of, Lee?" Fred asked.

"Not much of anything. The main thing I remember was the smell of him. It was awful—worst thing I've ever smelled. But the leg—it didn't hurt much—more like being pinched in a door."

"What happened then?"

"Well, the hunter with me shot again and you know I could feel the impact of that shot through the bear. I felt him stiffen for just a second. When that happened I crawled out from under him. He started after me but he was done for. He only went a little ways before he went down."

"Was your leg hurt badly?" I asked.

Lee shrugged, "Oh, it was a pretty good scratch."

"Yes, six inches long and to the bone," Alice leaned forward her black hair shining in the light of the gasoline lamp. "And he didn't tell me how bad it was. Not till he passed out did I get to see it and fix it up," she chided.

Lee grinned at her. "Didn't know myself how bad it was. I still don't think a bear'll come after you without a reason. This one was hurt. 'Course you don't want to mess with a mother bear and her cubs. Or come between a bear and his food cache. Or a mad bear. Thing is, you never know what's gonna make a bear mad. I knew a fellow once was killed by a mother bear. He was walking along and she just rose up from behind a log and attacked him. At first we couldn't figure it out but then we found one of her cubs had been eaten by a bear—probably a lone male. She went wild because her cub had been eaten."

"What would you advise us to do, Lee? We're usually so loaded down with camera equipment when we're taking movies, we can't carry firearms," Fred voiced a question we'd discussed many times.

Lee banged his pipe against his heel and thought it over.

"Well, *I'd* never go into the woods without a rifle but since you do, you ought to make plenty of noise so they'll know you're around. You don't want to take 'em by surprise. And if you do meet one, you shouldn't run. Just play dead and maybe all he'll do will sniff you or push you around a little out of curiosity."

These words of little comfort we were to recall with great vividness when we went into bear country to photograph the salmon run, but that was some weeks later. First we flew to Whitehorse and picked up our car to continue north over the Alcan.

PANNING GOLD

Chapter IX

UP THE ALCAN HIGHWAY

ALTHOUGH THE ALASKAN BORDER was only some 300 miles distant we were two days in making it for we found much of interest along the way. There were the snow covered Desadeash Mountains and there was 50-mile-long Lake Kluane looking as if it had been poured from a bottle of crème de menthe. On its shores was the Indian village of Burwash Landing with all the buildings made of logs including a neat little church, a corral for horses and a surprisingly modern two-story hotel. The most interesting attraction at Burwash, however, was the tavern keeper, 75-year-old Bert Cluett, whose flowing white beard brushed the top of the bar as he served his customers. Bert had been on his way from the States to Australia 50 years before when he had heard of the Klondike strike and had come north instead. He was still counting on going "down under" but not this summer.

"Nope, I'll be going prospecting again," he told us giving a meditative scratch to his neck. "Have somethin' looks pretty good. Have to pack in 35 miles . . ."

"By *yourself?*" we exclaimed.

"Yup," he replied ignoring our surprise. "Pays to go prospecting alone. That way you don't have to split what you get."

"So gold's what's kept you up here all these years?"

Bert gave the counter an expert swipe with a towel. "Yup. I'll hit it one of these days. All it takes is a little trying."

We wished Bert success in his 50th year of prospecting and bade him good-bye. The afternoon became increasingly warm as we drove.

"Must be near 100° in the sun," I had found the window-sill too hot for my arm.

Yet in a little over two hours we came to Snag where thermometers had registered as low as minus 83.6—the coldest temperature ever recorded officially on the North American continent. At a near-by lodge we struck up an acquaintance with the bus driver who had been on the Highway run that winter.

"Never missed a trip," he related proudly. "And I had plenty of passengers too because the planes weren't flying. We put up a wood burner in the bus just in case the motor quit but we never gave it a chance to—kept it going night and day. In the mornings, the tires would be frozen solid. It was like driving with a big rock imbedded in the tread, where the tire had frozen flat next to the ground. The thermometer never went above fifty below for twenty nine straight days."

"I remember," a soldier from near-by Snag airfield where the temperature had been recorded broke in. "It was so clear you could hear dogs barking five miles away. Why the nails in our barracks had frost standing out on 'em an inch and a half."

"That's so," the driver agreed. "On the night it hit the lowest, I couldn't get the bus to go over 28 miles an hour. Don't know why, maybe something to do with the oxygen."

We thought of these stories a little nostalgically when we crossed the border into Alaska on a day so hot our clothes stuck to the car seat.

Sunshine reflected off lakes scattered like mica in the vast spruce-covered flatlands. Expansive valleys webbed by glacial silt baked in its rays while the distant Alaska Range appeared silver edged against a cloudless sky. It was on this stretch we experienced one of the biggest thrills of driving the Alcan. We came to pavement. And though the heat made a layer of shimmering waves directly over it, we didn't notice, for we were rediscovering an almost forgotten pleasure—that of dustless, smooth riding. As if by magic, the squeaks and rattles which had accompanied us from the end of pavement out of Edmonton were suddenly gone.

Scrub spruce gradually gave way to birch and the country became open and rolling—entirely different from the close-in scenery of Southeastern. And then we were at Fairbanks, terminus of the Alaska Highway, "Golden Heart of Alaska."

Building was going on apace both in and out of the city—at the air force base and the International Airport, at the University of Alaska, on roads and houses, tourist courts and expanding businesses. Fairbanks was booming from the influx of itinerant workers, plus the summer's crop of tourists. Accommodations were as scarce as prices were high. Trailer camps mushroomed, laundromats were glutted with bundles of work clothes and people waited in long lines for their mail at the General Delivery window of the Post Office. With it all, there was a heady feeling of growth—of moving forward and doing new things and yet there remained traces of the old-time Alaska—in the open-heartedness of the people, in the easy credit of commercial establishments, in the log cabins scattered among many-storied buildings and in the prospectors who had been in the Gold Rush of 1912 from which Fairbanks had taken life.

We made a date with one of them—Johnny he told us to call him—to take his picture panning for gold. He was waiting for us when we arrived five minutes early next morning.

"Good morning Mr. and Missus."

"Good morning, Johnny. We didn't expect to see you out quite so early." We knew he'd been dancing until after midnight.

"Oh I've been up for hours."

"Meet any pretty girls at the dance last night?" Fred asked.

Johnny laughed. "A few. All married though."

We let the subject drop but Johnny kept thinking out loud. "Mighta married once myself but prospectin's no life for a woman. Some of my friends married and it never worked out. Women just don't understand how a man can feel about gold."

"If you had it to do over again would you do it differently?"

"Nope. I'd still do the same. Nothin' like good colors in your pan."

We left the city and drove north.

Johnny shook his head as we passed numerous truck farms and houses. "This was all birch and spruce forest when I first drove my dogs through here."

"You had a dog team?"

"Yup. Only way to get around. We used to look on our dogs as stock—like horses. Nowadays they're mostly raised for pets and racing—and I guess most prospectors are like me. They go into their claims and get supplied by bush pilots."

We came to the place where Johnny was to pan and all at once his easy-going manner was gone. The friendly blue eyes became calculating, his mouth a determined line. All business, he took up his shovel and gold pan and went directly to the creek. Shedding his coat and pushing his cap back on his white curls, he started dumping shovelfuls of gravel from the creek bed into his pan. Then squatting on the bank with the pan grasped firmly in both hands he began a washing process—a tilting of one edge to take in water, a gentle circular rocking to agitate the dirt, a careful sloshing out of muddy water, sand and gravel—over and over again.

"Look!" he was studying the bottom of the pan, eyebrows together in concentration.

There in a thin film of black sand were a half dozen flakes of gold and one tiny nugget no larger than the point of a led pencil.

"Not much," Johnny admitted. But this didn't daunt him nor did the fact the claim belonged to a friend and that it had been worked over four times already. The yellow in his pan told Johnny gold was there and because it was and for no other reason, he began all over again. Forgotten was the crick in his back he'd told us all prospectors "ended up with sooner or later."

Once he interrupted his work to press into use a small sluice box, a "long Tom" he'd spotted lying in the bushes. Though it was bleached gray by weather and missing one leg, Johnny was soon shoveling dirt into its slanting four-foot

trough. The bulk of it he washed away but the silt and gold
clinging to the canvas lining he gave a refined sluicing in his
gold pan. When the flakes numbered no more than would
come from half a turn of a pepper grater, we thought surely
Johnny would give up, but we were mistaken. It was nearly
two hours before we could persuade him to leave.

Before we did, he carefully took the flakes he'd panned and
wrapped them in a piece of paper. Then he borrowed a pen to
write a note.

> *"Tony*—Heres some you missed. Buy yourself some
> snoose. *Johnny"*

Grinning with satisfaction at his joke, he slid the packet
and note under the door of his friend's cabin. Then he was
ready to go with us to photograph the big mining operations
in gold fields near by.

Here we found subject matter offering dramatic and unusual compositions. There were the softly curved abstract
designs carved in the frozen earth by hydraulic hoses and
there were miles of hose looped like measuring worms to
to thaw pipes driven into the ground. Mammoth earth
movers swung their buckets high against the sky while dredges

floated in yellow mud lakes of their own making. Like giant monsters they would bite down to bedrock swallowing the earth and gravel into their clanking innards.

Johnny hooked his thumbs in his suspenders and gazed thoughtfully at the tons of screeching, pounding steel.

"That machine's doin' just what I do with my gold pan. It's shakin' the gold to the bottom and sloshin' off the dirt and gravel."

We followed his gaze to the rear of the dredge where the "sloshin' off" was taking place leaving a desolation of rocks and gravel known as tailings. Burnished by the late afternoon sun, they took on the appearance of rolls of gold coins stacked on end. It was an appropriate symbol of the wealth of the gold fields and with it, we completed our photography of mining except for the pouring of gold bricks which we took in Nome a few days later.

It was the Fourth of July weekend and we had made the flight primarily to get to the Eskimo dances and contests always held at the time.

Tony Polet, small, dark-eyed, white-haired trader who devoted his later years promoting Nome which he declared had "been good" to him, met us at the airport the afternoon of the 3rd.

"Hello, hello. You just in time for my granddaughter's birthday party." He showed us to a waiting taxi and directed the driver to his home. On the way, he pointed out a two-story imitation-brick-covered building. "New hotel, every modern convenience. Nome will be the greatest tourist center in Alaska. You'll see. We got the best Eskimo skin-sewers and the finest carved ivory you can buy."

We came to the main street, bordered on either side by board walks and squat frame buildings, some crouching behind elaborate false fronts. There was a bakery, an airlines office, a bank, Tony's store and an ice cream parlor named the "Glue Pot." At the far end, a water truck was making its deliveries. To our right, a curtain of fog rolled up from the Bering Sea just enough to reveal a freighter anchored far out and barges lightering supplies from it to the dredged channel of Snake River which Nome used for a port.

"We gotta new school and a big new hospital," Tony was saying. Nome was fortunate indeed to have such a man of vision as Tony Polet.

Tony's daughter, Mrs. Emily Bouchett was at the door to welcome us into a room attractively decorated with vases of wild flowers.

"More wild flowers grow around here than in any other section of the world except one small area in Switzerland," she told us.

The birthday party for Mary Jean was much like any little girl's birthday party anywhere except for one difference. When refreshment time came, Mrs. Bouchett appeared in the doorway carrying a large platter upon which rested not a cake but a watermelon with twelve glowing candles stuck in it.

"I always give her a watermelon for her birthday since she was a little girl," Tony smiled fondly at his granddaughter. "Sometimes it cost mosta' dollar a slice but it's always worth it." And there in that flower-bedecked room with Tony and the watermelon birthday cake was the essential spirit of

Nome—a fierce loyalty on the part of its residents who were completely individualistic, yet dependent upon one another for amusement.

We suspected the elaborate Fourth of July celebration was fully as much for the amusement of Nomites as for the tourists expected to flock in. Surely the participating Eskimos had more fun than anyone, both in the modern running races and in their own traditional contests of physical strength and skill.

There were kayak and umiak (large skin boat) races in the river channel. There was skin tossing from a hand-held walrus skin with the contestant going the highest in the air and maintaining his balance upon coming down proclaimed the winner. And there was the double kick—an amazing demonstration of muscular prowess. In this, the contenders kicked with both feet at a ball suspended above their heads and yet ended up with a powerful recoil standing on both feet. The winner couldn't have been over five feet three inches and the ball he moved had been hung by a man over six feet reaching well above his head. To top off the events, free ice cream was served to everyone and thoroughly enjoyed, despite the sleet which had begun to fall.

We found many other things of interest in Nome—the fine stitching of native boots and parkas, the Eskimos who came from King Island in their umiaks each year to carve ivory for the tourists and for local shops.

Within the week we were to be photographing another incident relating to transportation. This occurred on the lower Richardson Highway after we had returned to Fairbanks and picked up our car.

We had just come over a high mountain pass through low-hanging clouds and snow when we noticed a long line of cars and trucks on the winding road below. Even more strange was the reason for the hold up. At the head of the procession, a single seater airplane was being guided down the road by two men, one at each wing tip. Cameras in hand, we ran down to the plane.

"What happened?"

One of the men—tall, curly-headed and wearing mechanic's coveralls, grinned.

"I took the wrong turn. Instead of forking off on the Glen, I came straight on the Richardson. Too many clouds to get over the summit so I sat down on the road."

"Where were you coming from?"

"Pine Bluff, Arkansas. I followed the Alaska Highway all the way." He spotted my pencil and notebook. "My name's George Muschany," he added helpfully.

"Guess it's long enough here," the man on the other wing-tip stopped to study a straight stretch of road ahead, "but just so you don't clip a pole—" he went over to the tripod telephone poles paralleling the Highway and began methodically pushing them over.

"Who is he?"

"Ray Huddleston. He's with the Alaska Road Commission. When I landed, I found a Commission Relief cabin less than a mile away and telephoned for help. Well, guess I'd better give him a hand."

When the two men had tipped over enough poles to clear a runway, they came back to the plane and Muschany climbed in.

"I been in some tight spots flying in Arkansas but this Alaska. Man!" he started his motor and while we watched sped down the road and was airborne in a perfect takeoff.

"Guess you were a little surprised when he told you what had happened, weren't you?" Fred asked Mr. Huddleston.

He nodded. "Yes. This is the first time in twenty years with the Road Commission I've seen traffic stopped by an airplane."

As we drove past on our way to Anchorage we looked back to see Mr. Huddleston bending over and pulling the poles back in place.

That afternoon, we began to see game; first, a brown bear loping across the road in front of us just at dusk and the next day, a lordly moose, standing knee deep in a lake munching the pads of water lilies. I tried to creep up on him with my still cameras, while Fred was loading the movie cameras, but the moose felt other than in a picture-making mood. Looking vastly bored, he champed one more pad and with the faintest air of resentment turned and ambled into the woods.

My disappointment over not getting the moose was soon forgotten when we came to the Chugach Mountains, so wild and rugged, they looked as if they had exploded into being. Fred studied the exquisite patterns of dark and light formed by their uneven snow-covered planes and undulating glaciers.

"Those are the most paintable mountains I've seen in Alaska."

We followed the range for miles down the Glen Highway, sometimes getting a panoramic view across wide valleys splotched with lakes, other times crawling around their sides like an ant on a wall and always the view was magnificent.

Then, in late afternoon we came to the Matanuska Valley and here everything combined in an ultimate of scenic appeal. The Valley floor lay before us, large as the state of Rhode Island and tranquil in the blue haze of evening. It was completely surrounded by towering mountains shading from deep purple at their bases to peppermint-pink on their snow-covered tips. In the center was the village of Palmer with roads leading to farms cleared from forests of good-sized spruce, birch and cottonwood. Here and there lakes lay quiet and still or clear creeks hurried on their way to the river channel which meandered across the southern end of the Valley. At the head of the channel, one of the glaciers which fed it made a smooth, white path down and between the mountains. We stayed and watched until purple shadows had gradually pushed the pink up and off the peaks.

"That beats anything I've seen yet," Fred said. "Maybe this is it. Maybe this is where we should look for a place to build our home."

"Maybe."

We decided to come back and scout around as soon as we finished photographing Anchorage but that turned out to be nearly six weeks later. While in Anchorage we received word that the salmon run was on full tilt in Southeastern Alaska. We left immediately by plane. Selection of our future homesite could wait but the salmon run wouldn't.

CHAPTER X

THE SALMON RUN

WE STOOD ON THE BEACH at Olive Cove and watched Fish and Wildlife agent Dan Bates swerve his outboard motor boat in a final salute and disappear into the gray drizzle.

"He does love that boat, doesn't he?"

"Almost as much as steamed clams and homemade ice cream," Fred agreed. "Well, I guess we'd better get this stuff in out of the rain."

"Do we have to move it now? Can't we go see the salmon run first?"

"Sure," Fred looked up, glad I'd made the suggestion. "This can wait."

Hurriedly we put everything under a tarp and started toward Snake Creek. An odor of wet fish hung heavy as a fog bank and then we were at the creek staring incredulously into water brought to life by thousands of writhing salmon.

"They're packed thick enough to walk across the creek on their backs," Fred pointed to shoals so shallow the fish were halfway out of the water.

Farther up they would wrench themselves from the pack by twos and threes to leap in graceful arcs at a series of cascades, some to clear the first fall and proceed on their way, others to hit in water so swift they were washed back. The sound of flesh smacking flesh as they flailed against each other was punctuated by an occasional dull thud as one would charge head-on into the rocks. Now and then a fish would land on the banks to flop helplessly. Even as we watched, a large salmon plopped just a few feet from us. He was beginning to get thin from the long struggle and from lack of food, for his upper jaw was so hooked over the lower, feeding was impossible.

"I doubt that he'll make it but we'll give him a little help anyway." Gently Fred placed the fish in the water. For a moment the hump on his back cut the surface like a shark's fin and then he was one of the horde. We watched the run in silence, finding no words to express its magnitude. It was the most thrilling natural occurrence we had ever seen and the most affecting. We knew that the fish which finally fought their way to quiet water for spawning would have but a few hours and then an ugly end, lying belly up in the sun to be picked apart by the birds. This knowledge alone made their frantic efforts all the more poignant and magnificent.

It was dusk when Fred turned to go. "Guess we'd better establish ourselves at 'Bayview Manor'."

"Bayview Manor" was our somewhat grandiloquent name for a broken down one room shack at the head of Olive Cove. The rear end had long since caved in from the weight of many snows. There was no glass in the window openings and the single door sagged so determinedly we were unable to close it against a steady ocean breeze.

We stacked our tent, sleeping bag, borrowed rain togs, camera equipment and typewriter under a section of roof

which had miraculously retained all its shakes. Then, packing
a week's supply of groceries for four, we set out again. This
time our destination was a snug Fish and Wildlife cabin a
quarter of a mile up Snake Creek. It was dinnertime and we
were on our way to prepare a meal for the two young men
stationed there to count the salmon going upstream. In return
for furnishing their board for a week (except when we were
busy taking pictures) we were allowed the use of their cooking facilities—a pleasant and workable agreement we had
evolved to everyone's benefit. We had met the counters, Bill
Hoskins and Al Deershaw, earlier in the afternoon. They were
working this summer in Alaska to earn money to further their
education—Bill to start on his Doctor's degree, Al to finish
his last quarter of undergraduate work.

Al opened the door with a flourish, a big grin spread
between the beard and mustache he was cultivating. "Come
in. Come in and get warm." He motioned to the Yukon stove
complete with tiny oven in the back.

Bill uncurled from reading a book in his bunk. He was as
fair as Al was dark and shared his welcome.

"Hello. Did you get set up in the cabin?"

"Yes, we're all set at 'Bayview Manor.' " Fred shed his
pack of groceries and as he did so noticed a revolver lying on
the table. "Somebody been doing some target practice?"

"That's Al's," Bill said. "He's been practicing up in case
any of the bears start resenting our intrusion."

"Have you seen any?"

"Yes, all over the place," Al broke in. "They're out getting fish nearly every evening. That ought to make a good
picture for you."

"Yes, it should," Fred agreed. "Where's the sun in relation to the stream when they feed?" and he and the boys launched into a deep discussion on the best place and time to get pictures, while I cooked and served supper.

When we had finished eating, Al sat back and loosened his belt. "Whew! That was good. I'm certainly glad you came here to take movies. We were beginning to get cabin fever so badly we were counting slices of peaches as they came out of the can to make sure neither of us got more than the other." He stood up and put on his rain coat and hat. "Well, time to get to work. Want to see the weir?"

Fred and I assured him we did and hastily donned our rain gear.

The weir wasn't twenty steps from the cabin. It consisted of a barrier resembing a picket fence built across the creek with an opening in the center for the salmon to pass through. While we watched from the bank, Al made his way out on a catwalk to stand astraddle the opening. Through the misty twilight we could see hundreds of salmon like silver streaks

in the knee deep water. They would line up solid at the weir, gently nuzzling the slats until they found the opening and then bolt through like a rocket, but not before Al had clicked each one on his hand counter.

Bill came up beside us. "We counted 3,707 going through the weir in one morning the first of the week."

"You did! We'll want to be up early tomorrow if there's sunshine. I think we'll be going now."

"I'll walk down the path with you for a way. It's about twenty more minutes before my watch."

"How often do you change watch?"

"Every half hour. Mine will be the last one of the day."

We waved good-bye to Al and started out with Fred in front searching for the path with the flashlight. The forest was a waiting darkness—dense and oppressive. Towering evergreens made a roof against the fading twilight and what little light did penetrate was completely absorbed by the thick undergrowth. Though I was directly behind Fred, I found it necessary to feel my way along the soggy path and over slimy footlogs. The thick moss underfoot absorbed all sound except the muffled spatter of rain on the broad-leaved skunk cabbage. Then I recalled Lee Ellis' advice about bears, "make plenty of noise so they'll know you're coming."

"It's creepy, isn't it?" I asked in a much louder voice than necessary.

"Yes it is," Bill shot back just as loudly. "I should have brought Al's revolver."

"There's no point in your walking down with us and having to return by yourself, Bill. Sara and I can find the way all right and we have a flashlight."

"I guess you're right. I have to go on watch in a few minutes anyway," Bill turned to go. "Say, there's a strawberry patch down beside your cabin. We picked some the other day and they're awfully good. Well, I guess I'll head back."

We watched his flashlight stab the darkness momentarily and disappear, but long after he had gone we heard him whistling. A whistle didn't seem quite adequate protection to me. I felt there was much more likelihood of alerting the bears with full-voiced singing and straightway began a rousing rendition of "The Bear Came Over the Mountain."

"Shhhhhhh!" Fred motioned me to be quiet, and dropping to all fours, crept out on a rock promontory overlooking the creek. I peeped over his shoulder. Through the gathering dusk we saw a silhouette—a black bear busily fishing for his supper in a small slough about 100 yards downstream. With a quick, powerful swipe of his paw, he would scoop a salmon into the grass, lumber over to it and, tearing it into greedy mouthfuls, devour it completely. As we watched, another bear came out directly across from us. Where he stood, the salmon were so plentiful all he had to do was lower his snout into the water to come up with one between his teeth. With a sharp jerk of his head he would break its back, then turning, drop it on the bank. Instead of wolfing it down as we expected, he would sniff it fastidiously or perhaps take a few tentative nibbles and if it weren't completely to his liking, he would leave it to select and sample another.

"Just goes to show fishing's no sport when they come too easy," Fred whispered.

We crawled back to the path and to the repeated refrain of "The Bear Came Over the Mountain" continued on to "Bayview Manor." First we spread our sleeping bag in a corner where the least number of floor boards were missing. Then we hung our tent over the space where the rear wall should have been and finally nailed gunny sacks over the door and window openings. Thus fortified against the bears we turned in. Fred's even breathing told me he was asleep almost immediately. I was just beginning to drop off when I heard other breathing —a deep, heavy sniffing right outside our window. There was the rustle of huge bodies moving through deep grass and the vibration of heavy, cumbersome footsteps. I was paralyzed with fear, certain that these must be brown bears, for their movements sounded much too substantial to be the smaller blacks and certain, too, that they were heading directly to the cabin to make a meal of us, sleeping bag and all. Then I again remembered Lee's counseling. Of course!

"Boo!" I yelled sitting up. "Boo! Boo!" I repeated at the covered window. The reaction of the bears to these whoops issuing from the cabin remained undetermined but the effect upon Fred was immediate and spectacular. He must have jumped three feet into the air.

"What is the matter?"

"Bears," I whispered.

"Oh," he sounded relieved, though I don't know what worse my screams might have meant. "They're probably in the strawberry patch Bill told us about. Now lie down and get some sleep and don't *ever* yell like that again."

We resettled but neither of us slept too soundly for the thrashing and thumping continued outside the window until morning. With the first shaft of sunlight showing through the holes of our roof, we were up, and making certain none of our nocturnal visitors were still about, went out to the strawberry patch. We found several bear signs and that something large and heavy had been tramping around was evident though we could see no tracks in the thick grass.

We picked a rainhat full of strawberries and packing our camera equipment, went to the creek to set up where we had watched the bears fishing. Before the day was over, however, we had been up and down the banks of Snake Creek from "Bayview Manor" to the weir. The sun teased us, blazing like a searchlight one moment and dodging behind scudding clouds the next, giving us a total of only four hours of sunshine. Still it was time enough to get spectacular footage of the salmon leaping at the cascades and milling through the shoals. There had also been opportunity to study their behavior. We fancied that they leaped at the falls more frequently in overcast than when the sun shone and we were surprised to note they would not touch the bread we threw to them, though they were gradually starving.

This condition in no way affected their flavor we learned when we went to prepare dinner for our friends at the weir.

Al waded into the creek to bring up a plump, glistening salmon. There wasn't a flake left over when we had finished eating.

While I washed dishes, Fred loaded his cameras, Bill wrote a letter and Al worked on the charts he was keeping on the salmon run. A gentle rain began to tap on the roof but we didn't resent it. We were so cozy in the little cabin, it seemed appropriate. Had we known at the time how long it was to continue, we wouldn't have regarded it quite so poetically. That night marked the beginning of six straight days of almost constant rain. During that period, the sun shone for less than half an hour and even this was in stretches of five and ten minutes. In spite of it, we were able to complete our sequence of the salmon run and we were lucky on our pictures of bears fishing too. They had to be taken in overcast but as it turned out, this lighting approximated early evening, which was exactly as it should have been, since that was their natural feeding time.

In the middle of the seventh dripping day, Dan came in his outboard to take us to photograph the picturesque method of fishing known as purse seining. The commercial season on pink salmon was to open the following morning and Dan was on his way to see that regulations were observed by the fishermen already congregated and waiting at the mouth of Anan Creek. Dan's duties as an enforcement agent were temporary due to the increased work load of Fish and Wildlife personnel during fishing season. His usual work was in conservation, one pet project being the planting of salmon eggs in the headwaters of streams in his area. It was his hope the fish from these eggs, fertilized artificially and earlier in the season than normal, would return to their spawning waters before the regular runs started. This combination of research and being out of doors, Dan much preferred to policing the fishing fleet. However, if infractions were made, Dan would report them quite as conscientiously as he planted salmon eggs, for there was no compromising with Dan Bates when fishermen's aims were contrary to those of conservation.

It was completely dark and still raining when we sighted the fishing flotilla, gaily lighted as a carnival. Small green and red lights twinkled from the sides of the boats while balls and squares of yellow showed at every porthole and window. Here and there spotlights highlighted glistening decks or speared the bay in diagonal shafts of sparkling mist.

"Guess we'll give the boats a buzz to let them know we're here," Dan said cheerfully gunning the motor so there was no mistaking an enforcement agent had arrived.

When the fleet had been thoroughly alerted Dan turned toward the shore, a looming cliff in the darkness and as we came alongside, scrambled out and up the steep embankment.

"It's not very level but it's the best around," he called from somewhere above us.

Fred and I stepped ashore, stiff from the long ride, hungry and tired. We set to helping Dan put up the tarp for shelter and cooking a meal of sorts. The ground was so uneven we had to jack up one end of our gasoline stove with a skillet and when we started looking for a flat place to sleep we realized our campsite was on the side of a thirty-degree slope. After some scouting around we selected a spot under one corner of the tarp and retired, but sleeping on an incline was an art we had yet to master. We spent the night crawling up from the depths of our sleeping bag for air only to be met full in the face with a stinging rain for the wind had started to blow. The night seemed endless.

The next morning when we arrived at the fishing grounds we found all the boats busy with some waiting in line at the choicer spots. They made a lovely picture as they trailed out their nets and drew them together in a purse. We thought we were seeing a great many fish and we were but purse seining was a minor operation compared to the brailing done by a fish scow we boarded two days later.

The *Solo I* tended nine fish traps—labyrinths of wire fencing suspended from a floating framework of logs. As we came alongside, a net was dropped over the side into the trap and when it was pulled up, fish poured off into the scow bins in a torrent of quivering flesh and silver scales. Up until the last trap, the hauls had been a routine two or three thousand fish but on the last one, we hit what Captain Coulter described as "the jackpot." He did not tell us what the haul was but judging from the others, it must have been around seven thousand —so many that the load was taken down to Ketchikan because the local cannery couldn't handle it.

With fishing taken care of we flew back to Southwestern Alaska. The Matanuska Valley was even more lovely than we had remembered for now it was in harvest with fields turned to gold and the first yellow birch leaves breaking the forest green. During the next week, whenever our photographing was done, or on days of overcast, we spent our time searching out views.

"I don't believe we can top this anywhere." We had just rounded a curve and come head on into a view of Knik Glacier flanked by perpetually snow-covered mountains with Pioneer Peak dominating the Valley foreground. It was a scene we had caught again and again from various angles on different roads but always it was our favorite. "I think I could be satisfied to look at that for an awfully long time," Fred went on. "Could you?"

"Yes." In my mind I was seeing it centered in a big window with an attractive log studio home built around the window.

"Well then, that settles it. That's our view." Fred sounded enormously pleased and a little relieved. "Now, all we have to do is find a location we can see it from."

SEEGOO, THE SLED DOG

Chapter XI

WE FIND A HOME

FRED TURNED TO ME. "This is IT all right. We know we're on the highest ridge around and this looks like the highest spot on it to me."

We were in the middle of some 3,000 acres of wild ridge-land solidly wooded with spruce, cottonwood and birch. Though we could not see through the forest, we knew that a lovely little lake lay only a few steps to the right and directly below us for we had just come up from it. To our left, we visualized a panorama of the rugged Chugach Mountains once we had cleared, while to the Northwest the setting sun would light the sky behind the smoother, more regularly outlined, Talkeetna range.

Finding this perfect location had not been easy. There had been little specific information on open land at the Land Office and so it had been necessary to seek out settlers in the Valley to find what the situation was. There had been days of pursuing side roads, of many different heads shaking "no"— "no" the adjacent land was already taken up, "no" it was still under control of the Federal Government, or it was too inaccessible to be financially practical, or we would be unable to see the view we had decided we must look out on.

155

Finally our search had narrowed to the ridgeland, which, though only four miles from Palmer, had remained unsettled because it was unsuitable for farming. So we had acquired a map and a compass and started out on foot. Since no trails were cut through the forests, we had soon found a small axe for blazing our way to be a very necessary piece of equipment. It was late May and hot, mosquitoes were in their noisome prime and wild rose brambles scratched our faces and arms. Then after three long weeks we had found it—the place in all Alaska where we wanted our home—on the highest spot of a high ridge, overlooking a lake deep in the heart of Matanuska Valley.

"We'll build it of logs off our own land," Fred was saying, "and we'll have big windows looking out on the mountains and lake. Let's see now," he studied the compass, "one corner should face this way—"

The more we talked, the more enthusiastic we became.

"It's perfect—exactly what we want," I rhapsodized. "It's certainly worth all the days of searching."

"Years," Fred corrected. "Fifteen to be exact and some 70,000 miles of looking over Alaska."

We decided to apply for the land that same day but though we were in a fever to claim it for our own, the committee who was to consider our application was far from the same frame of mind. They did not meet for three weeks.

Meanwhile we went through an agony of wondering whether or not our application would be approved. We became dead certain that humanity at large was after "our" claim. Entertaining such suspicions, we grew secretive, meeting all direct questions with a blank stare and a vague shake of our heads.

We not only observed this peculiar transformation in ourselves but were reassured to find it in other would-be land-
owners later on.

The waiting period was an agony but it was not an idle one.

If we did get the land, it would be necessary to have a road
built into our homesite. This meant securing permission from
Gus Scheibl, through whose fields we would have to go to
reach the ridgeland.

Gus, one of the farm colonists of '35 who had enlarged his
original 40 to a 200 acre dairy farm, was understanding.
"Why sure, you can go through my land. I want a road to the
woods to get fuel anyway." So saying he signed an easement
sending us straight through his newly planted oats and peas.

Once we had our easement, we tentatively engaged Dave
Bryant to bulldoze our road in. Then we set about blazing
a trail for him to follow, for the site we had chosen was three
steep ridges over from the Scheibl farm.

The most important matter that concerned us, however, was
finding someone to help us with our log cabin. We soon
learned that log builders were scarce and it was only after
running down some half dozen leads that we finally ran across
a couple of experts, Art Koppenberg and his 23-year-old son,
Jerome. The evening we called on the Koppenbergs we didn't
have to be told that here indeed lived artists with an axe.
Their cabin was a masterpiece of wood sculpture, all hewn,
pegged and fitted by hand. With its low-pitched roof, wide
overhang and drooping eaves, it was a classic trapper's cabin.
Even though it was spanking new when we saw it, their cabin
had the look of belonging, of having "grown" with the woods.

"It's a beauty," Fred declared after introductions.

"Oh, it's nothin' much," Art ran his hand lovingly over the logs. "We had to put this one up in a hurry. Give us time and we do a real job."

Logwork was the love of Art's life. Before coming to Alaska he had been with the Forest Service in Minnesota and it was back there he'd won a speed-chopping contest against "all comers" in 1935. At one time, he told us further, he had chopped in exhibitions with Pete McClaren, World's Champion axe man from Australia.

As for Jerome, Art told us he was "perhaps the finest axe man I've ever seen. Ought to be—been at it since before he was long as an axe handle. . . ."

What more could we ask? We made up our minds on the spot. Would they build a cabin for us?

"Well I just wish we could. There's nothing we'd like better but," Art shook his head, "Jerome and me, we're working full time and they pay us awful good. Course we're not worth it, you understand but as long as they seem to think so—" he grinned, then his face grew serious as he thought some more. "Still I'd like mighty well to have another cabin in the Valley. About what size did you have in mind?"

We outlined our plans—one room 16 by 22 feet, with eight windows. Art listened intently, hunching over crossed legs, chewing on a sliver of spruce. When we finished he mulled it over for some time before speaking.

"Gee, I'd like to take that on. I'm just itchin' to pick up my axe again. Suppose you give us a little time to think it over. Maybe we can figure out a way."

With that half promise we left. When we called the following evening, they had made up their minds. They would undertake to build our cabin in the evenings after their regular jobs were done. This was made possible by the fact that daylight held until nearly eleven o'clock at that time of year. Barring "unforeseen circumstances" Art estimated the cabin might be completed by August first. The preliminary work of felling trees and skidding (pulling) them to our site, they would turn over to a friend, Grant Kinser. Art's other son, Sam, who was then on his way to Alaska with Mrs. Koppenberg and a daughter, would help too. We were to send for Grant and Sam the moment we learned our application had been approved.

We were jubilant. We felt like celebrating and so, the next day, we called a halt on work and went on a picnic—up a little used side road where we almost immediately stuck in a mud hole. In disgust we started for help little realizing that this mishap would indirectly lead to a great deal of future pleasure.

Cheerful, open-faced Lloyd King who pulled us out with his army command truck would accept no pay. "Shucks, if a man doesn't have time for his neighbors he's not worth much."

He did, however, accept a set of our books for his two youngsters and while thumbing through them mentioned having a husky pup which closely resembled some of the dogs in the illustrations.

Did he know where we could get such a pup? we asked.

"You can have the one at my house far as I'm concerned," he told us. "I'm just keeping it for a missionary. He got married recently and won't be mushing as much as he used to so he's getting rid of his team. I'll ask him about giving it to you. He's crazy about his dogs. Won't give 'em to anyone unless he's very sure they'll make a good home for them."

Could we see the dog?

"Why sure."

Our picnic forgotten, we followed Lloyd to his home and found what he had said to be true. The white sled pup who bounded toward the car in great awkward leaps could indeed have been Fred's illustrations come to life. He was only seven months old, yet he weighed seventy odd pounds and though gangling and gawky, we could see the possibilities of a really magnificent animal, for one day he would grow up to his tremendous feet. His block head, amber eyes and crescent tail already made a striking appearance.

When we left he gave an undeniable howl to go with us and we were just as reluctant to leave him behind, for he had gone straight to our hearts. Even before we reached Palmer, we had decided on a name for him—Seegoo, the Eskimo word for ice, since he had been born in December. From the first moment we saw him we talked as if he were ours and so, when word was passed along not a week later that the missionary had decided to give Seegoo to us, it was as if we'd known it all along. Though we didn't want to, we had to board him with Lloyd until we had a place to live.

As it turned out, we went for Seegoo in less than a week, for on June twentieth we were notified that the committee had accepted our application for "Lot 2, Section 7, Township 17 North, Range 2 East, Seward Meridian." That was what the paper said. We knew instead that we were now the owners of "forty acres of beautifully wooded knolls and shaded dells and one perfect sparkling lake."

Immediately upon hearing the news, we hurried over to tell

Koppenbergs they could begin work. The rest of the morning we set up our lean-to tent at the end of Gus' fields and began unloading our carry-all of the 1700 pounds of household goods we had brought up the Alcan including a wood burning range. Our mattress we would unroll in the back of the truck handily equipped with removable screens and curtains. We went in to Palmer and rented a post-office box and opened up a bank account. We put in an application for electricity. Before coming back out we bought a fifty gallon lard drum from the bakery to haul water in and a packing crate for a dog house. Then we went for Seegoo.

He was frantically glad to see us, licking the back of our necks and ears all the way to our camp. When we let him out of the car, he raced back and forth furrowing the air with sniffing. Once he was satisfied all was well, he flopped down beside the tent. He was "at home" and—so were we. Here we would live until the cabin was completed for we had no intentions of loading and unloading the range again until it could be carried over our threshold.

When Art, Jerome, Grant and Sam came that evening we all went in over the trail Fred and I had blazed. Even after rough walking over three ridges, the men managed to show enthusiasm, in their way.

"You sure got away from everybody," Jerome commented.

"Nice timber," Art ran an expert eye up and down a spruce.

"Well, if it's a view you want, you ought to get it from this ridge. It's certainly high enough," Grant sat down and fanned himself with his hat. "Can't see why anybody'd want to build on top of a ridge myself. 'Course for *your* purposes, a high ridge home's just the thing," he added hastily.

"High Ridge Home"—both of us caught and repeated the phrase. What a logical and natural name! Unwittingly, Grant had christened our home. Before long, it was shortened to simply "High Ridge" and "High Ridge" it remained. Thus the name for our home came into being long before the home itself. That night only the first cutting of the first tree for the clearing was made. I think the crew all felt what it meant to Fred and me, for there was no banter as Art chopped into a large birch. We heard it groan and saw it start to topple and not until then did Grant break the silence.

"Timberrrr!" his shout rang out and with it the quiet of the woods was gone at once and for always.

When we left around ten that night, Jerome drove his axe into a tree for Sam to use the next morning in falling trees.

"Aren't you afraid it will rust?" I asked.

"Well, if there's rust on it when I come tomorrow night, Sam gets fired," he replied. I needn't have worried. There wasn't a chance for rust to start. Sam did the full work of a man and Grant was a powerful and sure faller, in spite of a bout with polio which made it difficult for him to raise his hands to his hat brim. All the following week, they hunted out and felled prime spruce from our own land until there were 63 ready to be skidded once the road was 'dozed.

Art and Jerome lined out and laid the foundation of the cabin in the evening while Fred and I worked straight through both shifts clearing brush and trees. The days flew by, the stage of our building being made plain for us by what set of muscles were sore and where new blisters had developed.

On the evening of the 4th of July, Dave, the 'dozer man came with his 25 tons of steel and might to bulldoze our road. With a flourish, he lowered the huge blade and charged into the woods. At the first cut, our virgin forest somehow took on the aspect of a domestic woodland. In three and a half days Dave's road was to "High Ridge" but completion of the 'dozing didn't mean an end to our road building for now it had to be maintained. We filled sand spots with dirt and rock and then we filled dirt and gravel spots with sand. Driving in each day we conscientiously steered the truck "all over the road" in line with Dave's advice to avoid following the same ruts. We became so conditioned to doing this, we found ourselves going after rough spots far on the wrong side of the regular highways.

Once the road was in, we went to see Dale Nash about skidding our logs. Dale who was raising poultry and operating a small lumber mill on the side had put in three years flying the hump in India. Watching him jump his wheel tractor over fallen trees and slam through heavy brush, one could imagine he was squeezing every thrill possible from this land-based operation.

As the logs were skidded in, Fred and Sam rolled them up or "decked" them and I began peeling them, an easy task since the sap was up and the bark came off in long strips.

The really interesting part of our building began with the laying of the logs. For this, the Koppenbergs came armed with an assortment of tools they told us "hardly any carpenter today would know what to do with." One of these was a broad-axe, the outsized type axe usually associated with beheadings but which Jerome used to hew our four foundation logs into perfect halves. Before the fourth was laid we all wrote our names in the southwest joint and the date "July 20th," and now the actual log building began.

The first log of the second round was laid in place and inscribed with the contour of the log beneath. Then it was rolled off and this outline gouged out with the aid of a chisel and short handled sledge hammer, an axe, and an adze such as the Indians employed in their totem carving. After the first carving, it was put into place again for testing and remarking —always twice, frequently more often. The work was so exacting and required such a degree of skill that it often took Art and Jerome an entire evening to lay one log. This was with the help of Fred and Sam who were as yet novices but working hard to learn this technique.

The second log of the second round was barely laid before those "unforeseen circumstances" Art had mentioned began to materialize. It started raining and because the men could not "get a line" on a wet log, we lost one evening's work after another. Camping in this weather was miserable for with the rain had come a raw, biting wind. Food turned cold on our plates before we could finish eating, towels and clothes would not dry and crawling into our clammy sleeping bag at night was an increasing ordeal matched only by crawling out of it into the chill, gray mornings. Our road through Gus' field became a quagmire isolating us completely. We spent our days hunched over the range worrying about expenses which continued to go up although the cabin did not. The single most wearing feature, however, was the confinement of the tent. We were constantly bumping into each other or stepping on an uneven floor board which would pop up and overturn our orange crate cupboards. The only pleasant aspect of this weather was that it supplemented our water supply and we could allow ourselves two quarts of water for bathing instead of one.

At last, after seven straight days, the weather cleared but this didn't mark an end to our trouble. Art and Jerome's regular jobs began stretching into overtime cutting into their evening session at High Ridge. Then, one day, Jerome's work crew was sent North and he was out of the setup entirely. By the time work was started on the third round, the days had grown so short, Art could get in little more than an hour at a time and before the round was completed, his crew followed Jerome's.

Now it was up to young Sam and Fred.

Contrary to what we all feared, the cabin did not suffer at their hands. Being unsure of themselves made them all the more painstaking and this was the essence of good log building. Proficiency increased with every chip that flew and soon chips were lying half a foot deep. I abandoned my log peeling to bore peg holes for instead of using nails, our walls were braced with pegs which allowed the logs to ride down as they settled. With the sixth round, door and window openings were sawed and the cabin which had looked like a stockade began to take on the appearance of a house.

From that time on, our building went into high gear abetted by a phenomenal five-week stretch of sunshine. Another stroke of good luck was that Vic Yohn, an unfailingly cheerful trapper came to help us with the axe work. Then, the third week in August, Jerome returned just in time to supervise the installing of our window and door frames. It was a complicated operation since they were slid tongue in groove down

from the top—another measure for allowing the logs to settle.

The morning after our door frame went in, the Valley had a frost. We realized with a start that fall was upon us. At our camp, fireweed which had been a gorgeous fuschia spike when our logs were felled, had bloomed to its tip and was giving off its afterbirth of fuzz. In the field, Gus' oats and peas were grown and ready for harvest. Then, for the first time, new snow came to distant mountains. From the tenth round to the twelfth into the smaller logs of the gable we raced its steady descent into the valley. The day before the ridge pole "the best stick of them all" went in, we broke ice in our water barrel. But once the logs were all in place, the

laying of the roof seemed to go with incredible speed. We were to have three roofs, two of board covered by roofing paper with an air space between and a top one of cedar shingles. With the first roof down, we didn't wait for the other two. Golden leaves were pelting down on the scarlet mosaic of the low bush cranberries. It was time we were getting under a roof even if it was only a third completed.

On September 13 we transported the range from our base camp over the threshold of our cabin. We arranged our orange crate kitchen shelves, unrolled our mattress in a corner and set up a folding table and two chairs. The sea chest containing linens and winter clothing, we dusted off for company. We built a roaring fire using our log shavings for kindling and then we both dashed outside to watch the smoke curl up from our little chimney. There was no glass in the windows and no door and the roof was yet to be finished still after 85 days in a tent, it was 22′ x 16′ of pure luxury. Arm in arm we stood giving over completely to an exquisite feeling of achievement. Seegoo rounded a corner of the cabin and loped toward us, then, hearing a squirrel chatter in the woods was off to investigate.

"Well, guess I'll bring some water up from the lake," Fred started for the buckets.

"And I'd better light the lamp—"

And so life began at High Ridge.

WILDERNESS HOME

CHAPTER XII

LIFE AT HIGH RIDGE

SNOW FELL ON OCTOBER 10 and our forest, which had been picked clean by the fall winds, once more took on body. Overnight, the trees were fleshed while each spindly twig turned into a plump white finger. The silence was complete and nowhere was there movement—only the occasional noiseless dumping of its burden by a spruce bough. We were in a world apart. There was little time to enjoy it, however, for our roof had yet to be finished.

Immediately after breakfast Fred set to work, first sweeping the roof before he could begin to nail shingles. Though the snow was a hindrance to him, it was something I'd looked forward to a long time and for a reason. In clearing our forest and building, we'd accumulated a monstrous brush pile some 100 yards from the cabin. For weeks, we'd resisted lighting the unsightly thing for fear it might burn out of control. Our fall had been a dry one and the woods were like tinder. Already several bad fires had been reported in the Valley and this, added to the fact our cabin was a mile deep in forest, made us acutely conscious of the danger. Now with a two-inch snow coating the landscape, it seemed our chance had come.

In a happily incendiary mood, I went for matches and came back to light and throw one into the dry leaves which had sifted to the bottom of the pile. There was a minute wisp of smoke as they caught up—then nothing. The flame had gone out. I tried several more matches with the same result. In growing exasperation, I stuffed crumpled paper between branches and lit them. They simply flared up and burned themselves out, hardly marking the surrounding twigs. I called to Fred.

Giving the matter some thought, he suggested I use an old oil filter he'd taken out of the car. I did. It burned steadily and slowly and finally ignited the pile, but I began to realize that to keep a brush fire going required constant attendance. The limbs had to be laid one on top of the other and the fire fed by pushing yet unburned portions into the flame.

The sun came out and the snow melted and still it was

necessary to pile on fresh fuel. I began to wonder how the fires burned by themselves and got out of control.

We had a hurried luncheon—hurried because I was afraid my fire would go out—and then I was back, pulling brush, hacking limbs, lifting branches, and shoving them into the flame. In late afternoon Fred nailed down the last shingle, a momentous occasion, for this marked the actual completion of our cabin. It was cause for celebration, but instead, he eased his cramped knees down the ladder and began helping me keep the fire going. Even with the two of us working, the sun had dipped behind the opposite ridge and the first moose calls of evening were drifting up from the lake before our brush pile was completely burned. We were grimy with dirt and smoke and aching in every muscle. It was as hard work as we had ever done, yet all we had to show for it was a large gray scar burned deep in the ground.

Wearily, I started a fire in the range, not without a resentful thought of the heat that had gone to waste all day. Fred pushed himself up from his chair and went out to split wood. When he brought an armload in, his nose and ears were shiny red. "It's turning colder. Wind coming up too—looks like the beginning of a Matanuska."

A *Matanuska!* That meant wind directly off the Matanuska Glacier at the north end of the Valley, a freezing wind that might blow for hours or for days. We had heard of past Matanuskas—of how they forced fine snow beneath a door or piled drifts high enough to block a road. In a Matanuska, mighty spruce bent like buggy whips and one leaned forward to walk against it, or sometimes had to crawl. But, if we were marooned, if we couldn't get to the village for a week, we didn't care. While the forest around us might be lashed by fierce gusts, we would be snug in our cabin. Log walls that gleamed a taffy satin in the light of our gasoline lamp would shut out the cold; bright green and yellow curtains the winter's dark. Outside the air might be sharp enough to sear the lungs, inside were the homey odors of fresh spruce boughs, sprinkled and scattered on the floor before sweeping, and of moose steak cooking over a wood fire.

By this time our cabin was comfortably furnished. There was a box bed Fred had built, and if it lacked elegance with six-inch logs for legs and two-by-twelve inch boards at the head and foot, it was at least sturdy. In one corner we'd put up a clothes rack and above our range a shelf to hold our three-legged iron pot and flatirons. Beneath our kitchen win-

dow, orange-crate cupboards sagged with provisions—powdered milk and eggs, dried fruit and beans. Outside, a week's supply of stove wood was stacked under our overhang, and moose meat and slab bacon filled our food pit. Just two days before when we'd gone to Palmer to take showers at the public bath house we had brought back fifty gallons of water which we had siphoned into a drum inside the cabin. This method of getting water we'd found a great improvement over bringing it up from the lake, two buckets at a time.

With water at hand, we'd evolved a plumbing system. In our kitchen space we had hot water when the stove was going, cold water any time and a catch bucket made out of an empty oil tin. In our indoor washroom, in a corner behind the stove, we set up a washstand with an enamel basin and another catch bucket. The tending of these plus our gasoline lamp, chemical toilet, woodbox, trash and garbage cans had convinced us that a large part of pioneer living was made up of filling and emptying various vessels. There was still another filling and emptying Fred took care of, and that was gasoline and oil for the car. By buying a hundred gallons of gas at a time and oil in five-gallon cans, we realized quite a saving, although the first time Fred drained the car he opened the wrong valves and we had to hike into Palmer for a mechanic to repair the damage. But when Fred had changed the oil for a year, the difference had nearly paid our garage bill.

One luxury we allowed ourselves and that was a battery radio. Fred turned it on now, for the news. With detached interest we listened to warnings for residents of the village that there would be a power failure.

"Well, that's one thing we don't have to worry about."

"Nor the furnace going off or frozen pipes," I added.

"Think I'll let Seegoo in."

"Good."

Seegoo sporting his newly acquired winter coat was much more comfortable out-of-doors than in, but being of a gregarious nature, he would endure the warmth of the cabin to visit with us. Though he had been nine months old when we'd moved into the cabin and had never lived indoors before, we had never had to worry with housebreaking him nor with his chewing anything. A sharply spoken "no" was all the discipline necessary, since he was extremely susceptible to tones of voice. He seemed to sense what was correct canine behavior and to try to please us, and the gentle disposition he had shown as a pup remained even though he was almost grown and weighed close to 90 pounds.

He bounded in, tail flailing perilously near to the dinner dishes, and came to lean full weight against my knee.

"Where's Fred?" I asked.

Up went his ears. For a moment he looked questioningly at me, then went directly to the door to stand before it without making a sound. Begging or demanding was beneath Seegoo's dignity. With inborn gentility he assumed he would be waited upon—and he usually was.

As I let him out, a blast of wind hit us, slamming the door against the wall in a loud clap.

"Where are you?" I called to Fred.

"Here," his voice came from the darkness in the direction I had been burning brush. "I want to show you something."

I hurried over, walking backwards, pushing against the wind. "What is it?"

"That darn brush fire's gone into the ground. Look!"

Around the edges of the burned-out crater, sparks gnawed the earth like hungry red teeth.

I was horrified. A forest fire? Within a hundred yards of our cabin? And a wind blowing?

"What shall we do?"

"Pour water on it, I guess."

We hurried to the cabin to fill buckets, and bending under their weight groped our way through the smothering darkness. The wind was cruelly cold. Now and again the screak of a tree pinched in the fork of another tree or the splintering crack of large timber breaking before the wind would add their eerie notes to the din of the storm.

Back and forth we went, and not until the last spark was reduced to a resentful spit of steam did we call a halt and fall exhausted into bed.

During the night Fred went out to check the crater.

"How is it?" I asked when he came in, hair tousled from the wind.

"It's going again," he replied in a tired voice. "Evidently the water didn't sink in."

"Oh no! What will we do?"

"Get some sleep. I don't think it will flame up. It doesn't seem to be that kind of a fire. All it does is smolder in the ground. I guess the only way to put it out is to dig it back on itself."

And that was what we did—all the next day, and the next, and the one after that. We dug and shoveled until it seemed our backs would break and when we began to think we had the fire under control, another tree would topple over, its roots completely burned away. We came to realize that forest fires were not always spectacular or apparent. They could be skulking and insidious.

At the end of three days, the "Matanuska" died down and simultaneously we put out our fire for once and for all. Fred proposed we go into the village to get water, a suggestion I welcomed as a change in routine. The change proved to be one of form rather than substance. When we reached the foot of the first ridge, we found a tree lying across the road and from three days of shoveling we turned to chopping it away, plus the five others which had fallen across our road during the storm. Later we sawed them into lengths the two of us could carry to the cabin, and there we stacked them to be re-sawed into stove wood lengths, which Fred would subsequently split. Spruce was our favorite fuel because it caught up quickly, burned well and while burning gave off a wonderfully pleasant odor. Aspen produced a quick, hot flame, and birch was fine for steady heat but gummed the stove pipe with creosote, which we removed by throwing potato peelings on the fire.

For two weeks straight, the temperature fell to six below at night and never rose above twenty during the day. With this cold snap a comfortable vision, that of reaching out from our bed to light the fire each morning, ceased to be. As pleasant as it would have been to dress in a warmed room, we found it too chilly to stay up until the fire was out the night before in order to lay a fresh one for morning.

Frequently we awoke to find ice in our water drum and pitchers, and our windows opaque with frost. Though the range put out heat, it was a full two hours before the cabin warmed. This was because the space beneath the cabin had to be heated, as well as the room since the cracks which had developed between our floor boards made them about as air tight as a fire escape. Our fur boots felt good and several times I prepared breakfast while wearing my fur coat.

No more snow fell, but day after day our woods were transformed into silken lace by a shining coat of frozen fog. The crust of ice bordering the shoreline of our lake gradually converged toward the center. One morning we looked out to see a thin spider-web of ice covering what had been open water, and the next day the entire surface was frozen solid.

It would have been an ideal situation for creative work, but we were seriously handicapped by the lack of electricity as the days grew shorter. Our lamp was lit from the time we awoke until ten in the morning, when the sun finally rose above the mountains.

By mid-afternoon, darkness had come again. At best there were five hours of direct sunlight, two of which we spent sawing wood. We had reached a point of diminishing returns. With a reluctance that was a physical hurt, we decided we would have to leave High Ridge if we were to do our painting and writing.

On December 1, after filling the wood box and lamp and placing a jar of matches on the table, we locked our door for the first time since moving in. Snow was floating down in big, soft flakes, giving our beloved little cabin its most perfect setting. I started for the car and then, on impulse, turned to leave a kiss beside the door. "Wait for us. We'll be back."

Traveling through the States with Seegoo was fun but it was also complicated.

Riding, as he did, with his huge head outside a window, he looked for all the world like something that should have been mounted and hung over a fireplace. Small wonder, then, that autoists would drive alongside us on busy boulevards to ask "What is it?" or "Is he friendly?" Though it gave us a few uneasy starts in the beginning, eventually we became accustomed to police officers asking us to pull over "for a better look at your dog."

Now, our first consideration in choosing a hotel was whether or not it would take our dog. We found to our surprise that most hotels would.

We added yet another piece to our luggage to carry a leash, a long chain, dog food and dishes, and we became beggars of scraps at restaurants. Because of Seegoo, our days were made longer. We fed him in the evenings, after which he was taken for a walk. Unlike any sled dog we'd ever seen, he was a finicky eater, sniffing his food fastidiously, taking small bites, chewing them at length and otherwise dawdling for up to an hour. We wouldn't hurry him because we wanted to keep him in good condition and he knew it. Mealtime was his shining hour.

We took out liability insurance, although we never had to use it. Seegoo's disposition continued to be that of a "Ferdinand." We never knew him to snarl at anyone or attack a dog, but his size, while adding greatly to his appearance, was a serious handicap to his making friends, both human and four-footed.

We took pains to introduce him to the bell boys, elevator

attendants and maids so they wouldn't be startled, but sometimes there were slip-ups. Once we failed to remember our maid's day off, and when her substitute came in to tidy the room while we were out, she was so frightened at the sight of Seegoo she promptly leaped into the middle of the bed. Not only that, she proceeded to go through the entire bed-making operation from there, and once finished, was out the door in a second single leap.

Even though we might be gone from our hotel room for perhaps ten hours at a stretch, Seegoo never made any noise or otherwise betrayed our confidence. If, at first we thought this a poor life for a sled dog, we soon revised our thinking, for Seegoo loved show business and traveling.

In the beginning he had only a walk-on part before the lecture started—but he played it to the hilt. He would strut slowly and majestically across the stage, looking the audience over as much as to say "pretty good house tonight, but I had a better one in Waukegan." It was all I could do to hold him in the wings before his entrance, and when it was over I had to drag him out of the spotlight. One evening as I was making my few remarks about his age and size, he interrupted with a howl, to which the audience reacted with delighted laughter and applause. From then on, he incorporated this piece of business into his role, punctuating my every sentence with long and soulful bays delivered directly from center front.

He was a born trouper, not only in the theater but on television. At first, we had one small problem, for Seegoo, like all sled dogs, would lay his ears flat against his head when he was contented, and he was contented whenever his master was beside him. This gave him the appearance of a Polar bear rather than an alert, intelligent husky. With time, we found that his ears would perk up at the sound of crumpling paper, and as a result, most of the programs we appeared on were shot with one or more technicians standing by, wadding up balls of paper.

On at least one occasion, his ears went up without benefit of paper-crumpling and that was when our appearance followed a live animal act. We'd kept Seegoo outside the studio until the last minute, and when we did take him before the cameras we had to walk directly by a cage of white rabbits someone had overlooked. Seegoo sniffed, someone grabbed up the cage and—the top came off. White rabbits scattered in all directions. Seegoo went wild. Fortunately he was wearing a choke collar and Fred was able to hold him though visibly wrenched by each lunge. And so the show went on—an interview. Between questions, I admonished Fred out of the side of my mouth, "You're choking him to death."

"No, I'm not," came back in a loud stage whisper.

"Yes, you are."

I don't know how impressive any of the other shows we appeared on were, but I do know this one was remembered by at least one person. When we were downtown that afternoon, a complete stranger came up to us and remarked, "Oh, you're the couple whose dog chased the rabbits on television this morning, aren't you?"

Being known by our dog was a situation we came to accept. At first I had thought children along the streets were waving at us and would smile and wave in return. Then one day, my window happened to be down and I overheard them saying "Hello, doggy!" Friends invited us for weekends "—and be sure to bring Seegoo. The children are dying to see him." Wherever we went, Seegoo was followed by a coterie of admiring youngsters.

It was a happy time for our extraverted dog. Besides an excess of petting and the excitement of show business, he enjoyed traveling through the country lording it over the horses and cows confined to their pastures by fences.

Still in mid-March when Fred said, "We're going back to High Ridge, Seegoo, High Ridge, do you understand?" Seegoo leaped straight into the air—something he only did when he was overcome with happy expectation.

CHAPTER XIII

BEARS!

FRED TURNED OFF THE MOTOR of the truck. "It's no use. She won't budge."

We were mired in mud in the middle of a field we had to go through before reaching our road to High Ridge. I opened the door and Seegoo bounced out, a look of startled surprise spreading over his face as he sank to his chest in the mud. Gingerly we lowered our boots into the muck, down, down a foot before striking solid, frozen ground. "What in the world could cause such a mud hole?"

"Probably a snow drift piled against the fence last winter," Fred surmised. "Guess we'd better go for help."

We set out for young Rolland Grover's, our nearest neighbor since he'd bought the Scheibl farm the winter before. The fields were a quagmire. The spring thaw had started and already the frost had gone from the ground to a depth of four inches leaving a gummy, sucking sludge made the more impassable by a substratum of still frozen earth.

Spattered from head to foot, we reached Rolland's. Despite the fact he was resting, he cheerfully got into boots and went for his tractor. Fred and I climbed on the rear and back we rode to the mudhole in considerably less time than we'd left it. A strong chain was fastened to the two vehicles and the pulling began. The tractor cleats dug in, shooting a brown spray to the rear, the chain tightened to the breaking point, the truck wheels spun, but the truck itself remained exactly where it had been. Again Rolland gunned his motor, the tractor leaped forward and still the truck refused to move.

Such was the impasse when a farmer who happened to be going down the main road on a tractor saw our difficulty and offered his services. Now with two tractors chained to the front of the truck, the operation began anew. Motors roared, wheels churned, chains grew taunt and—nothing happened.

"I've a truck and a block and tackle," the farmer told us. "I'll go get those." Forthwith he was off, to return in a few minutes with the additional equipment and a son to man it. Our fleet lined up, two tractors, a truck and block and tackle and all pulled and this time most reluctantly the Matanuska mud yielded its captive.

We wanted to pay the men, an offer they flatly refused. When we insisted, they were equally insistent. "When we're in trouble you can help us," they said, and climbing on their respective conveyances drove away.

Fred started the motor of our truck. Magically we advanced, down the fence line to a corner, half around the turn and no further. We were stuck again! We looked at each other. The truck was still a mile and a half from High Ridge, but the afternoon was gone. The farmers would be starting their evening chores.

"Well," Fred said, "I guess we walk from here."

It was inconvenient. Still we weren't altogether unhappy about it. There was a certain thrill in knowing our comfort, our very subsistence, depended upon what we could pack in on our backs. This thrill we didn't intend denying Seegoo. We'd bought saddle bags for him from an Indian trapper on the trip up, and it was for them we looked first when we started digging through our baggage. To our disappointment, they were nowhere to be found. "Oh well, we can take enough for overnight," we told ourselves, and grudgingly added dog food to the toilet articles, portable radio and groceries we'd elected to carry.

Heavily loaded, we plodded through the fields, taking as direct a route as possible, while Seegoo taunted us by running far away in wide circles. When we came to the last stretch of road before starting over the ridges, we stopped in dismay. It was a chain of miniature lakes marking where snow had once drifted against the windrows.

"We'd never be able to get the truck through here," Fred shook his head. "Even the tractor wouldn't make those puddles."

"How long do you think it will take them to dry up?"

"No telling. It's just a good thing we have a supply of groceries in the truck."

The ridge road we found even less removed from winter, with up to three feet of snow filling it from bank to bank. This would have to melt before the earth beneath could begin to thaw, and once the thawing started there would be mud until all the frost had gone from the ground. While we glumly pondered the situation, Seegoo pranced past us, tail up, nose down, busily ferreting out the winter's accumulation of scents.

"Look at him. Isn't he Mr. Big, though?"

"Have fun while you may, old boy," Fred addressed him

directly. "Tomorrow you start packing, even though I may have to empty the truck to find your saddle bags." If this sounded dour it was because the dog food was getting heavy in our packs and walking over the ridges was proving a little tiresome. Though the crust on the snow was strong enough for Seegoo, it wouldn't hold us. We broke through at every step and made our way only by lifting each foot crab fashion, straight up, forward and down. The trees which had blown across the road in our absence were welcome resting places, still, our steps quickened as we started up the last ridge and then, with a flood of love, we saw our little cabin waiting staunch and lonely for our return. Now Seegoo knew he was home. Around and around the clearing he raced a dozen times in an exuberance of sheer delight.

Though past six in the evening, it was light enough to take off the shutters. Then, because our lake was still frozen, we filled our water drum with snow. With the wood we'd left stored in our woodbox we soon had a roaring fire going.

We fell into bed, promising ourselves a "sleep around the clock" but we failed to include Seegoo in this plan. Before five next morning, he'd routed us out with frenzied barking. Not twenty yards from him was a large female moose, hackles up, ears flat, squared off for battle. Slowly she lowered her head with a menacing glare toward Seegoo, chained beside his house. Fred went for the rifle, but before he could fire a warning shot, she had changed her mind and most deliberately turned and loped into the woods.

Now thoroughly awake, we decided to stay up, and besides, being at High Ridge again was so much fun that we couldn't waste time sleeping.

Immediately after breakfast, we were out looking over our domain. We found the snow gone except from the deeper glens, and already buds were beginning to break out on the birches and aspens. Without foliage the woods were more open and distances seemed much less. It was an ideal time for selecting trees we would take out to improve our view, but this had to wait for we were obliged to get more supplies.

On the walk to the truck we found, as we had expected, conditions getting worse instead of better. We probed the puddles with sticks and there was no bottom and the mud in the road was deepening by the hour. We gave up the idea of having the truck pulled out, and turned instead to selecting what we would need at the cabin. Before filling our own packs, however, we took pains to dig out Seegoo's saddle bags. The Indian trapper from whom we'd bought them had told us to fill them with bulky, light material until Seegoo became accustomed to his increased girth. This indoctrination we were forced to forego. Our staples happened to be heavy and compact and we were in no mood to carry Seegoo's food again, while he cavorted around us like a colt let out to pasture. We packed the bags, heavy and solid, and when they were ready we strapped them on him. To our astonishment, he accepted them without question. Except for an uncertain step or two before he found his balance, they did not seem to bother him at all. Contrary to the warnings the Indian had given us, he did not roll or try to throw them. The only noticeable effect was that he trotted just ahead of us, instead of roaming the country at large, as he had the day before.

Those first few days of being incommunicado at High Ridge we spent working in the woods. We became re-

acquainted with our squirrels and we were on hand to welcome the first returning woodpecker, who announced his presence by drumming a dead aspen. Twice more Seegoo awakened us barking at moose. By the week's end, green fuzz had begun to sprout on the bald, brown earth and surface water was forming on the lake, but when we walked down our road to pack in groceries and check the progress of breakup, we sunk ten inches in mud before hitting frozen ground.

Birds began to dart across the clearing, and the first yellow butterfly floated in on a warm south wind. The ice on our lake became so thin the color of the water showed through. Often we heard the honk of geese and looked up to see a flying wedge in the lingering twilight. The sun was putting in long days, rising at 3:47 and not setting until after eight. This sun, melting the snow on our ridge road, caused it to run in torrents and form large puddles at the foot of each grade. Soon two weeks had gone by.

During the third week, snow disappeared from even the deepest shaded ravine, and we started getting water where the ice had receded from the north shore of the lake. Almost overnight the opposite ridge was enveloped in a mist of green as buds turned into leaves big as pennies. For the first time, we didn't need the fire going all day and it became necessary to cache our food in a pit to keep it cool.

Now, when we hiked to the truck, we found the fields drying and checked like the pieces of a loosely fitted puzzle. On the ridge road the mud no more than covered our boot soles and the underlying layer of ice was gone, but where the snow drifts had lain, there remained mammoth puddles of water. When we tested them, they were still bottomless and shaking our heads we continued to the truck to fill our packs.

Gradually the shrinking island of ice on our lake disappeared entirely and a pair of loons took up residence to pour out their hearts in lonely calls at dusk. With spreading leaves, the woods once more closed in on us. The ground thawed enough for Fred to start digging a basement beneath the cabin. Surely summer had come, and it was time for breakup to be over—yet the mud where the puddles had been remained too deep to drive through. Not until after the first wild orchid bloomed were we at last able to get the truck out under its own power and projecting ourselves through the remaining mud in wild spurts of speed, skidded into the clearing at High

Ridge. It was May 18, five weeks and four days after our arrival in the Valley. Our retreat was at an end. With mixed feelings of regret and anticipation, we declared our summer season officially under way.

Now began the time for visiting—of guests from Anchorage to spend the day or Valley friends bringing home-made bread and fresh put-up jelly, of neighbors sharing our board and lending a hand with what needed being done. Another caller passing through the clearing might have gone unnoticed had Seegoo not announced it.

"It's a bear," Fred said, the moment he reached the window, "a big, black one."

It was part way down the ridge and out of sight from Seegoo, who must have detected it by scent or sound. Though the air was filled with sharp, excited barking, the bear showed no inclination to be off. It rose on its hind legs and standing slightly humped and off balance, sniffed the air intently.

Then it dropped to all fours, and while we watched open-mouthed, ambled directly toward the cabin. For a moment we were afraid it was going into the basement Fred had been digging, but instead it stopped at a birch tree just outside our window and once more stood up to look around. It was so close we could see its nose twitch, the quivering of the ears, even foam around the mouth.

"Look! Look!" Fred pressed my arm and pointed past the bear. "There's a cub!" Sure enough, spread-eagled on the trunk of a large spruce at the edge of the woods was a little cub. "I'd better bring Seegoo in. With that cub, she might be in a fighting mood." He took down the rifle and opening the door fired into the air.

While he dashed out and dragged Seegoo in, I watched the bear. At the sound of the shot, she had wheeled and started galloping toward the forest, but halfway across the clearing she had slowed to a stop, turned and reared up, gazing in the direction of the cabin. To our utter amazement, she advanced again, on to the base of the birch where she once more stopped, raised up and peered around. Though she squinted desperately, her eyesight was so poor she could not see us through the window.

"She looks frightened."

"That's why I can't understand her coming back——" before he'd finished, Fred's question was answered as a sudden bawling, loud and close, sounded from the birch where Mama stood. Then we saw it—another cub on a limb high among the leaves. At the first outcry, Mama looked up coaxing and cajoling her baby to come to her, but it was no use. Instead of his starting down, the first cub who had come to stand beside Mama, suddenly shinnied up. For just a moment, Mama pondered this new development, then having reached a decision, promptly followed suit.

"Great guns! Looks like we're going to have bears on our hands all day," Fred fumed. They did present a problem. A friend was coming over to help with the cellar, and a mother bear and two cubs up a tree beside the excavation wouldn't make for relaxed digging. As it turned out, we needn't have worried, for Mrs. Bruin took care of the situation. Having evidently delivered some effective threats, she presently descended, to be followed almost immediately by her wayward offsprings. With stern countenance, she watched them down and once on the ground, proceeded to herd them into the forest toward the lake.

We ourselves made frequent trips to the lake. Though a bath tub and unlimited quantities of hot water were made available to us by a friend "often as wanted, but Saturdays for sure" we liked to bathe in our lake whenever possible. Any warm day would find us lolling on the lake shore. On one such occasion, Seegoo suddenly bounded up, sniffed the air and was off, leaping like a gazelle through the tall grass. There was a scuffle followed by quiet.

"Seegoo!" we called. Up popped his head.

"Why he must have come across a bird." To me, his face appeared to be covered with white feathers.

He started toward us, and as he came closer our hearts sank, for we could see, instead of feathers, his face was stuck full of porcupine quills. Not only that, they were all down one side, covering both legs and even on his tongue and between his teeth. We tried to pull them out, but found we couldn't get hold of the sharp ends. There was nothing to do but take him to the veterinarian in Palmer.

Dr. Earl Graves and his wife and able assistant, Judy, set about the de-quilling. Seegoo never snarled once, though he was in such pain the Doctor shortly gave him an anesthetic. By the time the job was done two hours later we had begun a firm relationship with the Graves', the only good to come of the incident, for Earl warned us Seegoo wouldn't benefit by the experience. "If he'd been a pup he might think better the next time, but being a grown dog—he'll only be madder and more determined to annihilate the first porc that comes along."

Thereafter, though we didn't like to do it, we kept Seegoo close by us whenever we walked through the woods.

Seegoo had no sooner recovered from his bout with the porc than we were smack in the middle of another crisis, this time involving Fred and myself. It happened one morning. Fred was pulling brush at the edge of the woods when the air was suddenly filled with a pained "ouch."

"What's the matter?" I called through the window.

"A blasted yellow jacket got me."

"Oh, is that all?" I turned back to my washing.

"Ow!" came again from outside.

"Another one?" I inquired, without looking up.

"You're darn right. They're nesting somewhere near here. I'm going to town and get something to kill them."

"Must you make an extra trip? Can't that wait until we go after mail tomorrow?"

"*No.* I'm going now." And I knew there was no more persuading to be done.

The sound of the truck grew faint and ceased, and with it any further thoughts of yellow jackets. I finished my washing and went out to hang it up. Before I realized what was happening—wham!—my knee felt as if a red hot spike were being driven into it—and another and another. Screaming at the top of my voice, I raced to the cabin and shed my jeans, thereby releasing seven, maddened yellow jackets into the room. Bedlam ensued as I ran about thrashing my arms to fend them off; at the same time doing mortal battle with a folded newspaper. Once they were done in, I collapsed on the nearest chair, and though my knee was throbbing and swollen, I couldn't keep from laughing. Here was our home deep in the heart of 3,000 acres of forest, our nearest neighbor a mile and a half away and instead of shedding my slacks on the spot, I had very properly rushed indoors, to release my tormentors where they could do the most harm.

Needless to say, Fred received a hero's welcome upon his return from the "extra" trip to town.

For the next few days, when we were out clearing, we picked our way with extreme care, but as the hurt went from our stings, we gradually forgot the incident.

By now, our woods in the immediate area of the cabin were beginning to take on the aspects of a grove. We'd eliminated all the smaller trees. The bothersome stumps and large rotting logs had been pulled out by friends, who'd come to "do us a good turn" on their day off. Only the larger trees remained—the ones bigger around than both of us together. For them we needed a saw with deeper teeth than our Swede Saw, and so I was not surprised when Fred took me to Anchorage on my birthday and bought me a beautiful shiny cross-cut. It was a perfectly logical and much needed gift, but as I walked down the city's main street on three inch heels carrying a purse in one gloved hand and the cross-cut in the other, I had a feeling the passersby gave pause to wonder. My cross-cut was a joy to use. We went from one mammouth cotton wood to another making the mortal cut, watching it sway against the sky at length to topple exactly where we'd planned when we'd notched it to the lean.

Coincident with our clearing, the stack of logs beside the cabin reached healthy proportions. We proudly pointed them out to our neighbor, Rolland Grover, when he rode up on his horse with a box of fresh garden produce.

"You've got a good supply there," Rolland agreed, "but you'll be a long time sawing it into stove wood lengths. I've a buzz saw I hitch to my tractor. I'll bring it up some day and give you a hand."

Good as his word, he was up a few evenings later with his wife and another neighbor and in less than an hour, they'd buzzed a pile of stove wood which we would have been six months sawing.

Again and again, such neighborliness had been visited upon us. It had taken time, but eventually we'd learned that some things could not be paid for with money. Instead, we ourselves had turned a hand to fighting brush fires, pulling cars out of the mud and digging post holes. It was the way of the open heart. It went with the ready hand and the unlatched door, the deliberate step, the unfettered mind, the doing together in a new land—these things were Alaska. And these were the things we cherished, these and her matchless natural beauty.

Lake George was one. Hidden forty miles deep in the mountains, the fourteen mile long lake completely vanished once a year. Though the phenomenon had been known of for nearly half a century, less than a dozen persons had watched its disappearance first hand. We numbered ourselves among those twelve, when we made a three week's expedition there in late July.

ICE FALL, KNIK GLACIER

CHAPTER XIV

THE DISAPPEARING LAKE

"THERE IT IS!" Fred's voice rang with the thrill of realizing a five-year-old dream.

Through the windshield of the Seabee we gazed upon Alaska's fabulous Lake George. It lay in a valley fourteen miles long, four miles wide. To either side and straight ahead mountains rose abruptly from the water's edge while directly below, Knik Glacier formed a dam across the lower end. Seeing the lake, placid in the late July sunshine with icebergs floating on its surface like marshmallows, one would not suspect that it was even then bringing about its own destruction. But it was, and had been from the time the melting snows of late spring had given it birth.

Insidiously, in a small determined trickle at first, it had been gnawing an exit channel between Knik Glacier and an adjoining mountain. As the summer sun had shone long hours on the snow fields turning rivulets into torrents, Lake George had swelled, completely filling the valley and boring into its dam of ice with increasing pressure. Day after day, week after week, the relentless erosion had gone on until, at last, a five-mile-long passageway had been cut completely separating the glacier and the mountain. Once this was accomplished

the waters gushed unchecked, wearing away at the walls, undermining the ice above which began to cave in, ever widening the gap. We observed this cleavage when we'd flown in and we knew with its exit channel enlarging, the lake would soon reach its maximum disgorgement. As this took place the outpouring waters would do their utmost ravage to the glacier causing, in turn, a great sloughing off of its face. It was these ice falls we had come in to see, these and the dissolution and final disappearance of Lake George.

Our pilot, Les Green, circled past glaciers pendant at the throats of peaks or descending in ice lava to threshold on the water. "Looks like the wind's cleared a place to land," he said, and started down, down to meet our shadow, to speed past icebergs like lone freight cars on a siding and finally to settle in the water and taxi to a rock spit where Dr. Kirk Stone and Joe Richardson were waiting.

Fred opened the front half of the windshield. "Is anything going on yet?"

"It sure is. The lake's broken through and started to drain already." Kirk pointed to some small branches stuck into the lake shore at intervals. "Watch Seegoo doesn't knock those over. They're our record of how fast the water's going out—four to five inches an hour all night."

"No!"

Just then we heard a distinct peal of rolling thunder. Fred and I looked at each other in amazement. There wasn't the slightest sign of a storm.

"There she goes again," Joe cocked his head listening. "Must have been a big one that time."

Another clap sounded and we began to be aware of what it was—the accompaniment to Lake George's disappearing act. It was the crash of ice falling from Knik Glacier into the exit channel. Though the exit was three miles away the sound of the falls, amplified by the mountain directly opposite, seemed very close. No sooner had we realized this than we were in a turmoil to see the glacial pyrotechnics. Though their reasons were different, Kirk and Joe were just as anxious as we. Kirk, an associate professor of geography from the University of Wisconsin, was at the lake for scientific research while Joe, his guide, had become interested in glaciers through observing one in the back section of his homestead. With all of us agreed on wanting to see the ice falls as soon as possible our problem was getting to them.

The shoreline of the lake between us and the glacier was blocked by rock mountains sloping at a forty-five degree angle to the water's edge. We were left with two choices: one, to crawl along the rock cliffs; the other to go by Lake George teaming with icebergs. We decided to use both routes, a decision made possible since Kirk had brought along a rubber life raft. Already he had inflated it and gone on a trial run before we'd arrived. It was upon return from this maiden voyage he had given the raft a name—the "chip," surpassingly appropriate since it tossed on the water with an almost total disregard of its light aluminum paddles. Despite its shortcomings, however, the "chip" was held in high esteem by all of us because it would carry the equivalent of many trips backpacking. We began sorting the equipment, clothing and food we would need to set up our new camp at the head of the exit channel. Anything we could do without we placed under a tarp to await our return. Perishables were stored in a hole hacked in one of the many icebergs left stranded by the lowering lake.

Once this was done, we piled a load high about Kirk's six-foot five-inch frame and left him flailing the water while we set out on foot. The men were heavily loaded, Joe and Fred

leaning forward against the pull of seventy-pound packs while Seegoo and I carried thirty-five pounds apiece. Still, as we made our way up and around the sheer cliffs bordering the lake, the continuing boom of the ice falls caused us to hurry more than we would have ordinarily.

At first we tried to follow game trails but this didn't work out since they went higher and out of the way. Thereafter, we crawled along ledges so narrow we had to hold Seegoo because they would not accommodate his saddle bags. Though shale cut his paws and his bags hung up between boulders, his tail curling into a zero over his back indicated he was in his element. Far, far below, Kirk paddled in frenzied spurts of frustration pausing frequently to speculate whether he made more headway rowing or simply drifting with the current. He was giving the icebergs a wide berth and for a reason. Without warning one would suddenly disintegrate seeming to shatter from the core outward, spreading fragments of ice for some distance in the water. There was also the possibility of the bergs turning over as they became top heavy and scuttling the little raft with the first wave.

We hadn't gone very far before we discovered Joe to be an inexhaustible fund of information. When we would pause to rest, as we were frequently forced to do, something would "put him in the mind of" an amazing bit of woodlore.

"Now if you want to find direction, you take a straw and you hold it so's the cast shadow from it falls over the hour hand of your watch. Then, you take half the distance between that and twelve o'clock and it's south."

We also learned one could judge temperature by adding thirty-seven to the number of cricket chirps per fifteen seconds. You could only do this with male crickets, Joe went on to tell us, since they were the only ones equipped with "noise makers."

After two miles, we worked our way down to the shore and Kirk thundered in—paddles churning with the power of hummingbird wings.

"That blamed thing's simply not made for speed," he vowed changing off with Fred.

When we finally arrived at the lower end of the lake dusk had come. The exit channel was a yawning black chasm between us and the glacier face, showing in silhouette against the sky. We set up our camp on the lakeshore at the mouth of the channel and I began preparing supper on the gasoline stove. This was a convenience Joe held in some scorn. "A gas stove gives no comfort," he scoffed, building up a roaring fire of brush near by.

It was late, very late, by the time Fred and Joe started

leveling off the rocky slope for our tents, still, it seemed they finished in a short time. When I entered our lean-to I was surprised to see one third of the tent floor about a foot higher than the rest. "Why?" I asked.

"Two level," he informed me loftily. "Latest thing in pitching tents, you know."

Fred must have shared his idea with Joe for their tent was fashionably two level too. Evidently the rocks made for hard digging and it was late, very late.

Though we were tired we didn't sleep too soundly. There was an almost constant thundering from the gorge and both of us worried that all the ice would fall before we could get in to see it. At the first streak of light we were up and packing camera equipment.

Joe, meanwhile, had the efficient little two-burner going full force, melting ice gathered from one of the many ice bergs left stranded by the lowering lake. With his supply of brush depleted, he had found the stove offered some "comfort" after all. He used it further to fry bacon sliced "thick enough so's you could burn it on both sides" and the best flapjacks any of us had ever eaten. Thus fortified and with the sound of the falls booming in our ears, we started into the gorge.

We were hardly out of sight of our camp when we discovered the section of mountain opposite Knik Glacier was even more precipitous than that we had already come over. Before we could start into the gorge proper, it was necessary to go higher than the two-hundred-foot face of the glacier opposite. We crawled and pulled our way upward and as we did so, a mile and a half of the channel unfolded before us. We stopped to marvel at the gorgeous blues exposed along the glacier face when all at once, a single column as large and as solid in appearance as an eight story building separated itself from the wall of ice. While we watched incredulously, it leaned out and slowly settled across and into the water. A tremendous spray rose fan-shaped into the air as the sound of the splash reverberated through the gorge. The force of the display was stunning, almost terrifying at the same time, it was the most spectacular sight we'd ever seen. Yet it was only the beginning for great sections of ice continued to give way all along the glacier face.

We decided if we were to do justice to the phenomenon we

must photograph it from the bottom of the gorge. We cached what camera equipment we could possibly do without and began working our way forward and down. More than once we picked out a route only to have it dead end in a bluff straight up or a sheer drop, and then we came to a raging mountain waterfall. All along its course we toiled until at length we found a place at the base of one series of falls, at the head of another which we could span with a crude bridge of trees. This we took no chances on and roped ourselves across, but shortly after when we came to a wide trough of loose talus there was nothing to do except crawl on our hands and knees and hope we didn't start a landslide of our own. We began to realize why no more than twelve persons including Kirk and Joe and ourselves had gone into the gorge from this end during the break-out of Lake George.

It was nearly two hours before we were able to make a descent. When we did, it was at a place where the gorge took a sharp turn. Rising from the center of the bend was an oblong mass of rock and the action of the water around this rock, we were pleased to note, wrought greater devastation on the ice directly across than on any other visible section of the glacier face.

Once on the channel floor the falls were vastly more dramatic for the glacier loomed two hundred feet above us. As ice hurtled from its upper edge or slid in an avalanche off its face, the very earth seemed to shake. A few of the falls leaned across and into the channel as the first one we had seen and these were the ones we had to watch for in order to take cover. Not only could they reach us but the ensuing spray which looked so soft was filled with deadly ricocheting ice.

The sound of the falls bounding off the mountain behind hit us with a physical impact. There were ominous rumblings of shifting masses from deep within the glacier interspersed with the sharp crack of splitting ice and the artillery-like report of lesser pieces of ice falling from the top of the ice wall. There was the clack of ice rolling on ice and the tremendous roar when a section as long as a city block would give way in a cataclysmic severance. When this happened water plumed higher than the face of the glacier wall to reveal, as it fell, all the blues of the universe in the fresh wound of the ice.

Long after each dumping the waters would heave and regurgitate ice which would at length be regimented by the unyielding current of the outflowing lake. I thought such processions resembled the vertebrae of a snake. Fred, on the other hand, imagined a resemblance to task forces he had once watched in the Aleutians.

To us the falls were an emotional experience. We were humbled by their magnificence; at the same time we felt a deep exhilaration. Never had our searching after beauty been so well served as it was that day. And the three days thereafter for the extravaganza continued—with us the spectators and God as the playwright.

At the start the lake, discharging so rapidly it fell over a foot an hour, caused almost continuous falls off the glacier face. Gradually, however, as the volume of water decreased its force was lessened. The channel grew sluggish, losing its power to undercut and the glacier face began to assume a smoothly vertical appearance. There were fewer and fewer falls and then one day there was silence, pervasive and unbroken; a silence which would remain for a year until the glacier could once more advance against the mountain to form a dam and Lake George would be born again to perform its annual miracle of disappearing. The time had come for us to give attention to this miracle, this vanished lake.

We climbed one of the bluffs overlooking the lake bed. It was the eighth day and we saw the lake was truly gone, so completely in fact, we had difficulty remembering what it had looked like when we'd arrived. The upper part had shrunk to a shallow lagoon drained by a stream, while at the lower end all that remained were rock and silt flats. In the center, however, the lowering waters had left a spectacular aftermath. Moraine, emerging in a crescent around a feeder glacier, had formed a small lake and this lake choked with icebergs made a perfect vest pocket edition of the arctic ice pack.

The disappearance of the lake climaxing, as it did, a week of ice falls was almost too much to comprehend. We were left exhausted by the effort and more than ready for the rest a rainy spell provided. It began on a low key.

I awoke to the realization my eyes would hardly open they'd been so badly strained from the glare of the glacier in sunshine. Fred was not without battle scars too, his lips and face sunburned to a crisp crust. We crawled out of sleeping bags into cold, raw air, and pulled on clothing sticky with dampness. We came out of the tent to find the entire lake bed shrouded in ghostly, low-lying fog broken only by black islands of glacial moraine. Once proud icebergs perched incongruously on the steep banks a hundred feet above the lake bed. By this time they'd become rotten and from all directions we heard the sharp split followed by a many times amplified whisper that accompanied their disintegration.

Fred shuffled down to the smouldering fire Joe was laboring over, lifted a kettle of water and spilled half of it on the faltering sparks. Kirk hunched dejectedly over the smoke trying to get warm, the porkpie hat he usually wore at a jaunty angle jammed down to his ears. "What a day. I guess this means no mail drop," he predicted glumly. Seegoo with his coat matted as a soggy toothbrush was the most forlorn of all.

"Where's the wash water?" I asked, having finally forced my swollen eyes open.

Joe nodded—a little grimly I thought—to where Fred was absent mindedly filling the kettle with ice.

We ate our breakfast in gloomy silence though Fred did manage a wry smile when he nodded and the rain streamed off his cap bill into his food.

Then we heard it—the faint purr of an airplane motor closer and closer. When we turned toward the sound we saw a tiny red monoplane nosing out of the gray mist.

"It's him, it's Les," Kirk whooped and started running while the rest of us waved frantically to attract attention. Les made the mail drop on his first run and had disappeared in the fog before Kirk could bring the bundle back to the fire. Suddenly our aches and pains were forgotten as we poured over our letters, sharing portions with each other. Joe received of all things a pair of sun glasses and this in view of our sodden surroundings seemed roaringly funny. Before mail call was over we even found it in our hearts to laugh about Fred filling the warm wash water with ice—including Joe.

Once our dark mood was dispelled we stayed in good

spirits in spite of the continuing drizzle. We moved into Kirk and Joe's tent, that being the largest, and by keeping the gasoline stove going managed to be comfortable though quarters were a bit cramped. Kirk caught up on his tabulating sitting crosslegged by a lamp, Fred reclined Roman banquet style with his boots outside the tent flap.

We decided to move back to our base camp, a process which wasn't as simple as leaving it had been since we had no lake where we could launch the "chip." Still, we found hiking on the ledges marking former lake levels much easier than higher on cliffs. No sooner were we established than a wind storm hit.

It was still blowing the day Les came for us in the Seabee gliding to a perfect landing on the choppy waters of the lagoon. We loaded our equipment into the baggage section behind the two seats and then I climbed on top of it and called Seegoo who promptly leaped in to recline across my lap. Les and Fred took their places in front, we waved good-bye to Kirk and Joe, the motor was revved and in a mighty roar we started taxiing across the lagoon. With gathering speed and a crescendo of sound we left the water but then, something happened. The plane dropped like a rock. Another gun and we were once more air-borne only to plunge again striking the water harder. A third and a fourth time the Seabee leapfrogged through the water going higher, plummeting farther and harder. I saw Les lean forward and grip the controls, tenseness in every line of his body. Fred involuntarily lunged to help the plane "over the step" while Seegoo, sensing disaster, climbed over me in a frantic effort to keep from falling. The next attempt we smacked the water with a punishing, concussive wallop. The whole fuselage shuddered. There was a splintering crack and the windshield shattered. I pressed toward the side window and watched horrified as a float ripped off. "This is it," I remember thinking but in so doing, I failed to give Les the credit he deserved as one of the best bush pilots in Alaska.

Making a split second decision he cut his speed and then, with consummate skill he began guiding the crippled Seabee through treacherous swells toward shore. After the longest minutes Fred and I had ever lived we felt the welcome scrape of the plane's belly on the beach. We all scrambled out to stand looking at each other, too shaken to say a word. The air was deadly calm, the only sound a gentle lapping of water until Kirk came running toward us.

"Nice work, Les," he shouted heartily but as he drew near, I could see his face was gray as were both the other men's. Down the beach Joe was launching the "chip" to retrieve the pontoon which was bobbing in the water.

"Well, guess the thing to do's get the plane on land," Les decided.

Just then the slightest puff of wind came up. Before we realized what was happening the Seabee went over, the unsupported wing digging into the water and spinning the fuselage around and down. Kirk and Fred made a jump for the other wing which had tilted above their heads and by swinging full weight from it brought the plane horizontal again. I couldn't help but shudder to think what might have happened had that puff of wind come moments earlier.

Once the Seabee had been pulled up on the beach, we could see it was in bad shape. Not only was the float gone and the windshield broken but the force of the crash had burst out some rivets and the bottom was split open. A water takeoff was now impossible. Les decided instead to take off on wheels by himself and return for us in another plane the following day. Before that could be done, however, an emergency airstrip had to be cleared on the newly exposed lake bed. This the men set about doing; carrying rock and rolling boulders in spite of a blizzard of fine sand which enveloped them as the wind came up again. Four hours later they had cleared an eight hundred foot strip which Les pronounced satisfactory but it was two more hours before the wind died down. When it did, everything except just enough gasoline to make the forty mile flight back to Palmer was emptied from the Seabee, then Kirk, Joe and Fred took their places as human markers along the improvised runway. Les climbed into his plane, zoomed down the strip and was airborne in much less than the eight hundred feet. Up he climbed, past timberline which had become a fringe of burnished rust in the late afternoon sun; up, until the Seabee was only a speck against the lavender peaks. Only then did he give us the salute we were all waiting for—a reassuring dip of the wings and not until we saw this, did we turn our dirt-lined faces from the sky and breathe a sigh of relief.

"It was close, wasn't it?"

"Yes, it was," the strain still showed in Kirk's eyes. "When I saw the plane porpoise like that, I thought uh oh—"

"I knew you were in for trouble when the wind stopped the *eggzact* minute you took off," Joe recalled, "and there were those big swells and no wind for lift—"

"You were in the air before you had flying speed because

the water literally dropped out from under you," Kirk further explained.

"We were!" I looked at Fred but he had stopped listening. Instead he was gazing at one of the perpetually snow-covered peaks whose jagged surface was a purple blue pattern of light and shade. "Look at that mountain," he exclaimed.

Obligingly Joe turned to study the sheer planes and overhanging ledges. "She'd be a mean one to get up, I'd think. Plenty of chance for snow slides—"

"Now *that's* something I'd like to see," Fred responded enthusiastically. "Avalanches! I've heard of a place on Mt. McKinley . . ."